# CHICAGO CUBS
## YESTERDAY & TODAY

## STEVE JOHNSON

Voyageur Press

First published in 2008 by Voyageur Press, an imprint of MBI Publishing Company, 400 First Avenue North, Suite 300, Minneapolis, MN 55401

Voyageur Press titles are also available at discounts in bulk quantity for industrial or sales-promotional use. For details write to Special Sales Manager at MBI Publishing Company, 400 First Avenue North, Suite 300, Minneapolis, MN 55401

Library of Congress Cataloging-in-Publication Data

Johnson, Steve, 1965-
  [Chicago Cubs yesterday and today]
  Chicago Cubs yesterday & today / by Steve Johnson.
     p. cm.
  Includes index.
  ISBN 978-0-7603-3246-7 (hardbound w/ jacket)  1. Chicago Cubs (Baseball team)—History.  2. Baseball players—United States.  I. Title.
GV875.C6J654 2008
796.357'64097731—dc22
                                    2007034683

*On the front cover, top left:* Joe Tinker, circa 1910 (Transcendental Graphics/The Rucker Archive); *top right:* Carlos Zambrano, 2007 (AP/Wide World Photos); *bottom:* Wrigley Field, 2007 (photo by Andrew Woolley).

*On the frontispiece:* Cubs logo, 1950s (Transcendental Graphics/The Rucker Archive).

*On the title page, main:* Wrigley Field, 2004 (AP/Wide World Photos); *inset:* Ernie Banks, 1960s (Transcendental Graphics/The Rucker Archive).

*On the back cover, top left:* West Side Grounds (*Chicago Daily News* negatives collection, Chicago Historical Society); *top right:* Wrigley Field (AP/Wide World Photos); *bottom left:* Billy Williams (National Baseball Hall of Fame Library, Cooperstown, NY); *bottom right:* Aramis Ramirez (Jeff Gross/Getty Images).

Editor: Josh Leventhal
Designer: Maria Friedrich


Printed in China

# CONTENTS

# ACKNOWLEDGMENTS

To bring together all the best of more than 130 years of Chicago Cubs history was a considerable challenge—and far beyond me to attempt it alone. I owe a great debt of gratitude to several people who made this book possible, and a lot of fun, as well.

Many thanks to Josh Leventhal of Voyageur Press for his expert baseball wisdom, which provided inspiration at all the right moments, and for the editorial lifeline that kept me afloat. Josh and the whole Voyageur crew have been a genuine pleasure to work with.

Researching the storied Cubs ball team demanded the very best sources with the inside take that only devoted fans can provide. Neil Finnell was incomparable in his efforts to help make this project a success. His www.chicagocubson-line.com website is one of the most comprehensive Cubbies resources out there.

Art Ahrens, a loyal fan from way back and a superlative writer in his own right, helped to launch the book from its earliest chapters. It was a privilege to work with Art and learn from his knowledge of and passion for the team.

Dan Clemmerson provided more superfan research help as deadline pressure loomed like a full count in the bottom of the ninth, particularly for the chapters on the team's all-time greats.

My family's enduring patience, as always, makes it all happen. Much love to all of you.

And to the fans: Your devotion to the Cubs for generations is staggering, and I hope I succeeded in providing the proper celebration of this beloved team. With the franchise's long and distinguished history, it was difficult to decide which classic story or legendary player to set aside for another time—but many of the best are here. I join you in a salute to the Cubs and a long and winning future. See you at the World Series!

# PHOTO AND ILLUSTRATION CREDITS

We wish to acknowledge the following for providing the illustrations included in the book. Every effort has been made to locate the copyright holders for materials used, and we apologize for any oversights. Unless otherwise noted, all other images are from the Voyageur Press collection.

**AP/Wide World Photos:** p. 2, 10 left, 19 bottom right, 22, 23 both, 25 both, 30 bottom, 32 bottom, 33 both, 35 top right, 35 bottom, 39 both, 41 bottom left and bottom right, 43 bottom right, 45 bottom right, 47 bottom, 49 bottom, 51, 53 bottom, 56 left, 61 bottom, 63 bottom, 67, 71 right, 75 all, 79, 81 bottom right, 82, 85 right, 86 top right, 88 top right, 92 both, 93, 95 all, 107, 109 bottom, 110 right, 111 top right, 114, 115 top, 119 bottom, 121 bottom right, 122 bottom, 125 both, 127 top, 129 all, 130 bottom, 131 bottom left and bottom right, 132 right, 133, 136 top right, 137 bottom right, 139 all, 140 top, 141 both.

**Chicago a News negatives collection, Chicago Historical Society:** p. 11 top (SDN-006862), 29 bottom (SDN-058902), 32 top (SDN-065930), 34 (SDN-061299), 46 (SDN-052543), 55 left (SDN-069283), 65 bottom (SDN-054439), 69 top (SDN-054748A), 69 bottom (SDN-069827), 77 left (SDN-055785), 78 bottom (SDN-061557), 81 top (SDN-002899), 84 bottom left (SDN-052340), 104 (SDN-008822), 110 left (SDN-069129), 112 (SDN-060311), 116 left (SDN-059393), 118 bottom left (SDN-005881),120 (SDN-051369), 121 top (SDN-068127), 121 bottom left (SDN-065777), 124 bottom left (SDN-054408), 126 (SDN-009808), 127 bottom left (SDN006014), 128 top (SDN-054400), 131 top (DN-0007669).

**George Brace Photo Collection:** p. 41 top, 43 top right, 72 top, 91 top left, 97 bottom left, 113, 116 right, 117 top left and top right, 119 top, 124 top right, 128 bottom, 134 both, 135 top, 135 bottom left, 136 bottom left.

**Getty Images/Jonathan Daniel:** p. 11 bottom, 115 bottom, 135 bottom right.

**Getty Images/Rich Pilling/MLB Photos:** 88 bottom left.

**Inzerillo, Tony:** p. 45 bottom left.

**Library of Congress, Prints and Photographs Division:** p. 13 top, 17 top, 20, 64, 91 bottom, 94 bottom, 100 top.

**Library of Congress, Prints and Photographs Division, George Grantham Bain Collection:** p. 24 bottom, 26, 35 top left, 44 bottom left, 54 right, 77 right, 84 top right, 86 bottom left, 98 bottom left, center, and right.

**McCormick, Michael:** p. 70 bottom, 101 bottom left; 50 top, 83 top right, 99 top left, photos by Lou Sauritch; 137, photo by Michael Ponzini.

**National Baseball Hall of Fame Library, Cooperstown, N.Y.:** p. 9 top, 14, 16 right, 19 bottom left, 28, 30 top, 36 left, 47 top, 49 top left, 58, 60, 61 top left, 62, 66 bottom left, 105, 108 both, 127 bottom right.

**Ponzini, Michael:** p. 57 both, 83 bottom left.

**Shutterstock:** p. 89, 101 bottom right, photos by Todd Taulman; 111 bottom, photo by Frank Tremmel; 117 bottom, photo by Jenny Solomon.

**Smith, Don:** p. 99 top right.

**Tringali, Rob, Jr.:** p. 50 bottom, 53 top, 71 left, 99 bottom left.

**Transcendental Graphics/The Rucker Archive:** p. 1, 3, 8 both, 12, 15 top, 16 left, 17 bottom, 18, 19 top, 21 all, 24 top, 29 top, 36 right, 37 both, 42 both, 44 top right, 48, 49 top right, 52 both, 54 left, 55 right, 56 right, 59 both, 63 top, 66 top, 68, 72 bottom, 73 both, 76 both, 78 top, 80, 85 left, 87, 90, 91 top right, 96 both, 97 top right and bottom right, 101 top, 102, 103 top, 106 top left and bottom left, 118 right, 122 top, 123 top right, 132 left, 138 all.

**Woolley, Andrew:** p. 109 top.

**Yablonsky, Bryan:** p. 27 bottom right, 83 bottom right, 99 bottom right.

# CUBS YESTERDAY, CUBS TODAY

With lineage that traces directly to the Chicago White Stockings of the old National Association, today's Chicago Cubs have the longest continuous tenure in one city among all major league franchises. Indeed, organized baseball in the Windy City dates back even further, to amateur clubs of the 1860s.

The White Stockings club was first organized in 1870, and that September they journeyed to Cincinnati to test their mettle against the world's first professional baseball team. The Cincinnati Red Stockings, who boasted a two-year tally of 113 wins and only a handful of losses, were shocked by the upstart White Stockings, who secured a 10-6 victory. The Red Stockings ventured to Chicago a month later for a rematch, were beat again, and the scene was set for what would become one of the most revered clubs in sports history.

It seems only appropriate that the establishment of organized professional baseball—of the sport as we know it today—featured Chicago as a major influence. In 1871, the National Association of Professional Base Ball Players formed with the Chicago White Stockings as a charter member. The Chicago club was leading the championship race that first season, until disaster struck. That October, the Great Chicago Fire reduced much of the city, including the White Stockings' ballpark, to ashes. While Chicago focused on rebuilding, the team faded from the league until 1874, when they rejoined the National Association for what proved to be that league's final two seasons.

*Chicago White Stockings, 1871*

*Chicago White Stockings, 1886*

*1984 East Division champs*

During the 1875 season, White Stockings owner William Hulbert convinced Boston's star pitcher Albert Spalding, along with three other Boston standouts, to jump to his team for the following season. The move not only proved instrumental in returning Chicago to its winning ways, it also led to the creation of a new league, the National League of Professional Baseball Clubs, in 1876. The White Stockings dominated the National League's inaugural season and won the 1876 championship. The team's good fortune continued during the 1880s, led by new manager and star first baseman, Adrian "Cap" Anson, as Chicago captured five league titles between 1880 and 1886.

After the turn of the twentieth century, a new baseball dynasty emerged in Chicago. The fabled double-play combination of Joe Tinker, Johnny Evers, and Frank Chance and a formidable pitching staff helped to secure four more pennants and back-to-back World Series titles (1907 and 1908). Fans were delirious. They watched games from rooftops, hanging over fences and from lampposts, and packed into the ballpark.

In 1916, the Cubs moved into a spiffy new home at the intersection of Clark and Addison streets—a site that would become hallowed ground for Chicago baseball fans. Over the subsequent

decades, the broadcasting of games on the radio and, most importantly, the accumulation of five more National League pennants between 1929 and 1945 carried the franchise to new levels of popularity.

As the nation entered the postwar decades of prosperity and progress, the Chicago Cubs and their fans were headed for lean years. After hanging 10 National League pennants from the

*Wrigley Field, Chicago*

rafters in a span of 39 years (1906–1945), the team would go another 39 years before it again played postseason baseball—and 62 years (and counting) without a trip to the World Series. Indeed, in 20 seasons from 1947 to 1966, the Cubs posted a record above .500 only once, and they never finished higher than fifth place in the standings. The long, long dry spell earned the Cubs the "Loveable Losers" nickname, but Chicago fans remained dedicated to their team.

By the end of the 1960s, the club had assembled a collection of all-stars and future Hall of Famers. With Ernie Banks, Ron Santo, Billy Williams, Ferguson Jenkins, and others, the Cubs compiled six straight winning seasons from 1967 to 1972 while finishing no lower than third place.

All four Cubs legends had departed by 1975, but a new wave of stars would follow: Bruce Sutter, Ryne Sandberg, Rick Sutcliffe, Mark Grace, Andre Dawson, Greg Maddux, and more. Division titles in 1984 and 1989—the team's only winning seasons between 1973 and 1993—generated great enthusiasm among the Cubs faithful. The club broke the two-million attendance mark for the first time in 1984. But the "Lovable Losers" only flirted with the postseason, never managing to make the relationship last.

By the late 1990s, the power explosion offered by Sammy Sosa at the plate and hurlers Kerry Wood and Mark Prior on the mound brought star quality, and another division title in 2003, to the Friendly Confines of Wrigley Field. Attendance has topped three million for four years running, through 2007, as the eternal optimism of long-suffering Cubs fans remains strong.

Critics and fair-weather fans are always quick to point to the six-decade drought in World Series action for the Cubs, but baseball is much more than chasing a title. The Cubs and Wrigley Field are part of Chicago's character, part of its people, and the fans packing the stands for generations are rightly proud of this storied franchise.

Still, the year 2008 marks the one-hundredth anniversary of the last Cubs World Series victory. Feels like a good time to bring another one home.

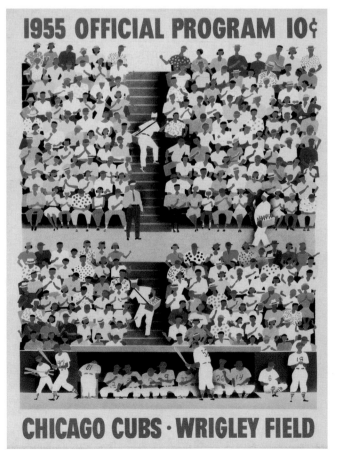

*Cubs scorecard, 1955*

*An ever-optimistic Cubs fan, 1998*

*Chicago Cubs raise the 1907 world championship banner, Opening Day, 1908*

*Wrigley Field, Opening Day, 2007*

# LEAGUES AND TEAMS

During the formative years of the sport of baseball, amateur teams from around the country competed under loosely defined regulations and schedules in the 1850s and 1860s. In 1871, professional clubs from the East Coast and Midwest got together and established the National Association of Professional Base Ball Players, or National Association, as the governing body. The Chicago White Stockings were one of nine clubs to play in the league that first season, although the team had to bow out before the season was completed due to the Great Chicago Fire later that year.

Chicago rejoined the league in 1874, but the National Association was fraught with franchise turnover, scheduling problems, rampant gambling, and drunkenness. Midway through the 1875 season, owner William Hulbert signed Al Spalding to a secret agreement to play for Chicago in 1876. He then lured Ross Barnes, Cal McVey, and Deacon White from Boston to do the same and went on to nab the young Adrian "Cap" Anson from Philadelphia. Hulbert knew that the other owners might try to expel him and his club from the National Association for his actions, and so he conspired to establish a new league. In February 1876, he convinced the teams from Boston, Chicago, Hartford, New York, Philadelphia, and St. Louis, and independent franchises from Cincinnati and Louisville, to join him in a new National League of Professional Baseball Clubs. Hulbert vowed to clean up the improper behavior sullying the game and to bring economic stability to the league and greater profits to the owners. A month later, the National Association disbanded.

The National League was not without its instability, however, and by 1880, Chicago was one of only two franchises, along with Boston, still in its original city. The White Stockings were left to face a string of newcomers from Providence, Buffalo, Troy, Worcester, Cleveland, and elsewhere.

The host cities continued to shift throughout the 1880s, but the National League remained an eight-team operation until 1892. Four teams from the short-lived American Association jumped to the NL after that rival league folded in 1891. In 1900, the league retracted back to eight teams, and those same eight franchises constituted the National League for the next 62 years.

*Chicago White Stockings and Troy Haymakers, National Association, 1871*

The addition of two expansion clubs in 1962 did not do much to lift Chicago out of the bottom of the standings during the first few years of the 10-team league. In 1969, with the creation of two more expansion teams, the league split into two divisions, East and West. Chicago was lumped into the East with New York, Philadelphia, Pittsburgh, St. Louis, and Montreal—and the Cubs found themselves in the second position in the division in three out of the next four years.

Teams shifted around again 25 years later, when the now 14-team league was realigned into three divisions in 1994. Chicago was matched up with more geographically correct cities in the NL's Central Division: Pittsburgh, Cincinnati, St. Louis, Houston, and later, Milwaukee.

Since the inception of the National League in 1876, the Chicago franchise is the only one of the inaugural eight still operating in the same city.

*Twelve-team National League, 1895*

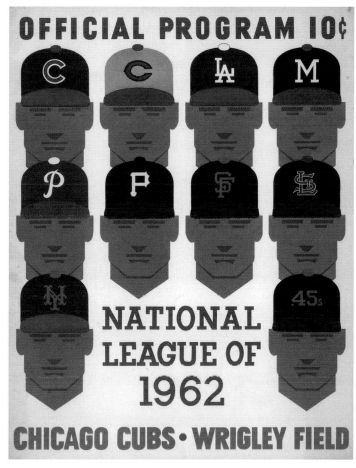

*Ten-team National League, 1962*

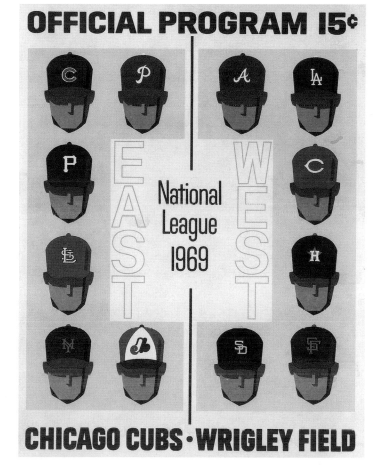

*Two-division National League, 1969*

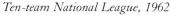

# THE NAME GAME

In the early years of National League baseball in Chicago, fans might have had a difficult time keeping straight what to call their team. The club had three "official" names before settling on the Cubs, and they went by more than half a dozen other nicknames at times.

It was easy in the beginning: The team wore white hosiery as part of the uniform, so White Stockings was a logical fit. (Officially, they were simply the Chicago National League Ballclub.) The White Stockings name held from the club's inception through the 1880s—even when the team briefly switched to black socks later in the decade, at which point they were variably referred to as the Black Stockings or Black Sox.

When many of the team's biggest stars departed in the late 1880s, manager Cap Anson was left to skipper a roster full of youngsters. The fresh-faced bucks were branded the "Colts,"

and the name soon extended to the whole team. The franchise went as the Chicago Colts for most of the 1890s.

Anson put in 22 seasons as a player for Chicago, and he doubled up as the manager for 19 of them. He had become a kind of father figure for the team. When Anson was fired in 1898, observers tagged the club the Orphans, which name stuck through the 1901 season.

Other monikers were used in the papers and by fans to describe the Chicago National Leaguers around the turn of the twentieth century. In 1898, a string of early-season rainouts led to the Rainmakers nickname. For spring training in 1899, the team headed to a New Mexico ranch and included horseback riding in their training routine; that season they were referred to by some as the Cowboys or Rough Riders. In 1901 and 1902, when the American League emerged as a legitimate major league, many players defected to the new league, leaving behind a skeleton crew in Chicago—and thus, the nickname Remnants was used by some observers for the 1901 season.

Finally, in the March 27, 1902, issue of the *Chicago Daily News*, an article previewing the rebuilding ballclub noted that manager Frank Selee would be devoting "his strongest efforts on the team work of the new Cubs this year." The name was a hit with fans. Still, some sportswriters continued to try out other names, such as the Panamas, after players wore Panama hats during 1903 spring training in Los Angeles; the Zephyrs, in homage to the team's speedy players and Chicago's windy reputation; the Nationals; and the Trojans, for Johnny Evers' hometown of Troy, New York.

The Cubs name was officially recognized in 1907. Manager Frank Chance urged the media to use the catchy title, and in that season's World Series the team received new uniforms with a large white bear on the sleeves. One hundred years later, the Cubs they remain.

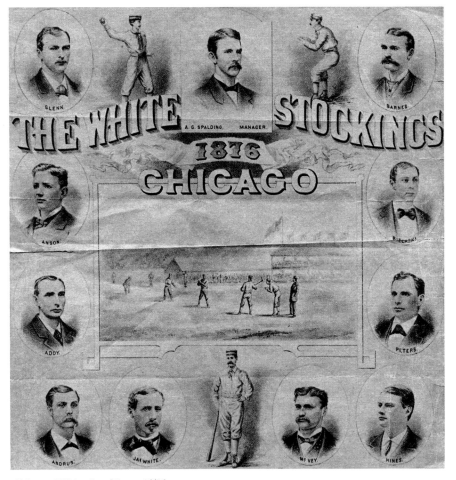

*Chicago White Stockings, 1876*

*Chicago Colts, 1890*

*Chicago Cubs, 1908*

# THE GREAT TEAMS AND THE DYNASTIES

Looking back at the franchise's performance over the last 130-plus years, the "Loveable Losers" nickname may be unjustly bestowed. Since the inception of the National League in 1876, no franchise has won more baseball games than the Chicago Cubs. Their all-time winning percentage is surpassed by only five major league franchises (Yankees, Giants, Dodgers, Cardinals, and Red Sox). One hundred years may be a long time to wait for a World Series title, but consider this: From 1876 to 1945, Chicago posted a combined .559 record, and the list of accomplishments during that 70-year span is impressive:

- 51 winning seasons
- 16 pennants or league titles
- 10 World Series appearances
- 2 World Series championships

When William Hulbert raided the National Association's Boston club of its top players in 1875, he formed a foundation for success for his White Stockings. Pitcher Al Spalding led the way with an impressive 47 wins in 1876. Second baseman Ross Barnes contributed a league-high (and franchise record) .429

batting average, one of four White Stockings among the league's top five hitters. The offense averaged nearly three runs per game more than the next most-productive team. Simply put, Chicago dominated. The team finished with a record of 52 wins and 14 losses to bring home the franchise's first championship title.

Chicago dipped to fifth place in 1877, and most of the stars from the championship squad were gone by the end of the decade. They still had Cap Anson, however, who continued his superb play. In 1879, the 27-year-old first baseman took the managerial reins as well, and the arrival of Ned Williamson, Abner Dalrymple, George Gore, and Mike "King" Kelly helped to build a veritable dynasty in Chicago. They barreled to the pennant in 1880, recording a 21-game win streak along the way. Gore and Anson finished first and second in batting average.

More titles followed in 1881 and 1882, making Chicago the first "three-peat" champion in National League history. Anson's crew put another notch in the dynasty belt in 1885 and added one more a year later—giving them six titles in the first 11 seasons of the National League. The 1886 White Stockings

*1876 World Champion Chicago White Stockings*

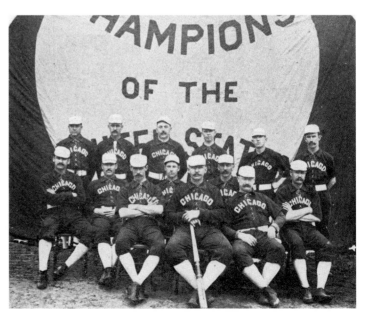

*1886 World Champion Chicago White Stockings*

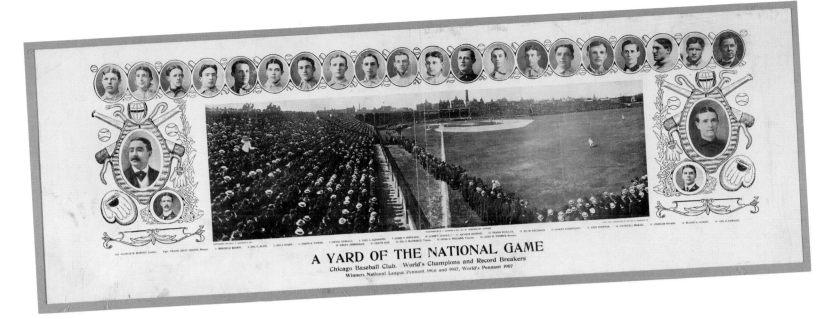

*Ballpark and roster of the 1907 World Champion Cubs*

became the first 90-win team in major league history, finishing with a 90-34 record.

The Chicago Cubs of 1906–1910 rightly deserve inclusion in any discussion of baseball dynasties. The star-filled crew grabbed four pennants in five years and became the first team to win back-to-back World Series (1907 and 1908). The Cubs posted an astounding .693 winning percentage over the five years, an all-time league record. In 1906, they went 116-36, establishing a record for wins in a season. The one time they failed to finish atop the league standings, in 1909, the Cubs won 104 games only to finish six-and-a-half games behind Pittsburgh—thus setting another, if more dubious, record for most wins by a second-place team. While the infield trio of Tinker, Evers, and Chance inspired poems by sportswriters, the Cubs' dominating pitching staff led the league in earned run average four times in five years.

While the Cubs had moments of brilliance in the years following the golden age of 1906–1910, including a pennant in 1918, the assemblage of stars that came together at the end of the 1920s made Chicago a consistent contender. In 1929, veteran superstar Rogers Hornsby joined a nucleus that included Gabby Hartnett, Charlie Grimm, Hack Wilson, and Kiki Cuyler. The team won 98 games that year and earned another trip to the Fall Classic. Hartnett and Grimm remained with the club, as players or

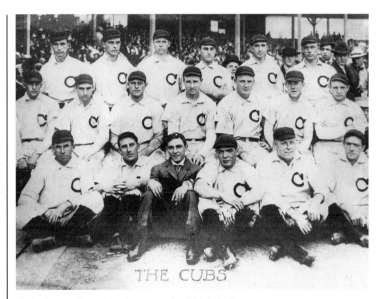

*The beginnings of a dynasty: the 1905 Cubs*

managers or both, for three more pennant seasons—1932, 1935, and 1938—alongside a new crop of young stars, such as Phil Cavarretta, Stan Hack, Billy Herman, and Lon Warneke. The 1935 crew notched 100 victories and catapulted to the pennant with a 21-game win streak in the season's final month. They clinched it by sweeping the St. Louis Cardinals in a doubleheader on September 27.

Many will point to the 1969 squad as one of the best, if also disappointing, teams in franchise history. Leo Durocher signed on as manager in 1966, promising winning changes for the team. Boasting a roster that included Ernie Banks, Billy Williams, Ron Santo, Glenn Beckert, and Don Kessinger, his pledge had substance. The Cubs finished third in 1967 and 1968 and seemed on the fast track to winning the division in 1969. They held the top spot in the standings for most of the season, only to fade when it counted most. Their 9-game lead in mid-August gradually eroded. After dropping 11 of 12 games in early September, they were sunk. Chicago finished 8 games behind the New York Mets in the National League East. Second-place finishes in 1970 and 1972 were as close as they would get for another dozen years.

The emergence of Ryne Sandberg and the acquisition of veterans Gary "Sarge" Matthews, Dennis Eckersley, and Rick Sutcliffe in 1984 produced the franchise's winningest season in four decades. The 96 victories reflected a 25-game turnaround from the previous season. Sandberg was named the National League's Most Valuable Player, Sutcliffe brought home the Cy Young Award, and Jim Frey won Manager of the Year. The team's first postseason appearance since 1945 ended in disappointment, however, as the team dropped the final three games of the National League Championship Series. By the end of the decade, Sandberg and Sutcliffe had been joined by a veteran star in Andre Dawson, a hitting sensation in Mark Grace, a pitching phenom in Greg Maddux, and Rookie of the Year Jerome Walton. The combination generated another 90-plus-win season in 1989—and another postseason flop.

Those two division titles, plus a Wild Card berth in 1998, were isolated diamonds in the rough of many losing years. It wasn't until the new millennium that Chicago was able to put together back-to-back winning seasons, accomplished under manager Dusty Baker in 2003 and 2004.

A strong showing in 2007 marked the fourth winning season of the decade. The talent-laden lineup featured only one survivor from the 2003 division champs, third baseman Aramis Ramirez, but the addition of all-stars Derrek Lee and Alfonso Soriano, and a solid pitching staff spearheaded by Carlos Zambrano and Ted Lilly, propelled the Cubs to the top of the Central Division standings and a third postseason appearance in 10 years.

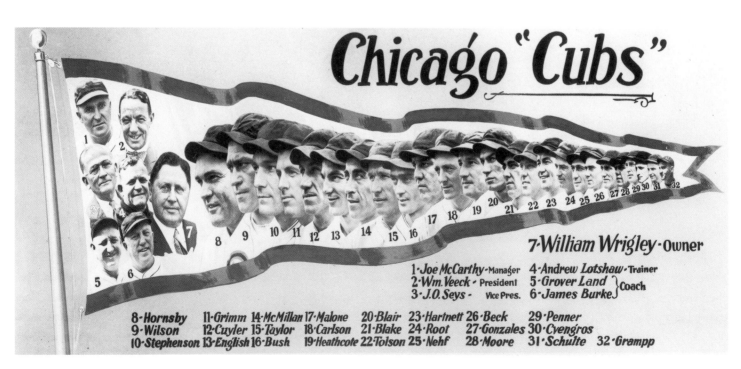

*1929 Chicago Cubs*

*The Cubs about to celebrate clinching the 1935 pennant, in St. Louis*

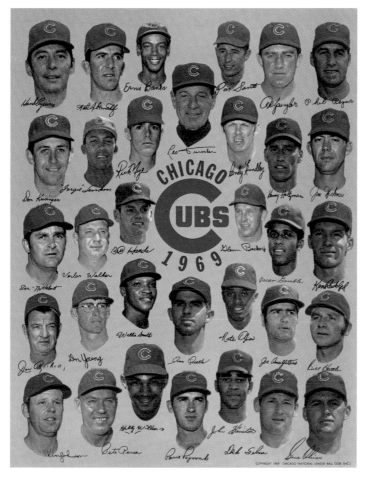

*1969 Chicago Cubs*

*Alfonso Soriano and Derrek Lee celebrate clinching the 2007 division crown*

*Game Two, 1907 World Series, West Side Grounds, October 9, 1907*

# CHAMPIONSHIP SERIES

The modern World Series between the National League champions and their American League counterparts was not established until 1903, but its precursor can be found in the 1880s, and the Chicago club was a frequent participant. Following the 1882 season, the NL-champion White Stockings agreed to play the champions from the newly formed American Association, the Cincinnati Red Stockings. It was the first championship competition between teams from different leagues in baseball history. Only two games were played, each team won one, and the exhibition series ended in a tie.

Chicago's titles in 1885 and 1886 were mirrored by back-to-back American Association titles for the St. Louis Brown Stockings. The opening game of the 1885 championship series ended in a tie due to darkness. Controversy followed in Game Two when St. Louis walked off the field in protest of an umpire's ruling; Chicago was granted a forfeit win. The teams split the next four games, and St. Louis won the seventh and final game. Once again, Chicago's postseason outing ended inconclusively, with three wins for each side and one tie. In the following year's rematch, the conclusion was clear, but not to Chicago's favor. St. Louis won the 1886 series, four games to two.

The Cubs were also a fixture during the first decade of the modern World Series. The record-setting 1906 squad, which won 116 regular-season games, faced their crosstown foes from the American League in the postseason. In baseball's first intra-city Fall Classic, Chicago fans packed the Cubs' West Side Grounds and the White Sox's South Side Park in chilly October weather. After alternating wins through the first four games, the "Hitless Wonders," as the Sox were known, pulled out wins in the final two contests to clinch the upset victory.

The Cubs' consecutive pennants in 1907 and 1908 led to consecutive series match-ups with the Detroit Tigers. Chicago dominated, losing just one game over the two years. The Cubs pitchers allowed only four earned runs in 48 innings during the 1907 series, and they closed out the 1908 series with back-to-back shutouts. It proved to be the last time the revered club would win it all.

In five of its next seven trips to the World Series, Chicago faced off against historic dynasties from the American League. In 1910, the Cubs managed just one win against Connie Mack's Philadelphia Athletics, winners of three World Series from 1910 to 1914. The Boston Red Sox secured their fourth world championship of the decade by besting Chicago in 1918. Connie

Cartoon postcard of 1907 World Series results

1938 World Series program

1910 World Series program

Game One, 1929 World Series, Wrigley Field, October 8, 1929

Mack's rebuilt dynasty in Philadelphia of the late 1920s kicked off another championship streak with a four-games-to-one series victory over the Cubs, in 1929. Two of Chicago's pennants in the 1930s were rewarded with postseason dates with perhaps the most dominant team in baseball history—the New York Yankees of the 1930s—and each time, the Cubs were swept. In 1932, Chicago posted the worst team ERA in World Series history (9.26). The nail in the coffin of humiliation was Babe Ruth's fabled "called shot" in Game Three.

In 1935 and again in 1945, the Cubs battled their old nemeses from Detroit. Although Chicago opened both series with shutout victories, they came up short in the end. Little did the Cubs faithful know that the Game Seven loss to Detroit at Wrigley Field on October 10, 1945, would be their last taste of the Fall Classic for . . . well, who knows how long.

# THE CURSE OF THE BILLY GOAT

Once the Boston Red Sox shed the "Curse of the Bambino" and the White Sox broke free from the "Curse of the Black Sox" with their respective World Series victories in 2004 and 2005, Chicago Cubs fans stood alone in their prolonged frustration. While the front office has made some questionable decisions over the years, and the players themselves made some costly errors, it is a goat that is often cited as the explanation for the decades of misfortunate.

The "Curse of the Billy Goat" was actually invoked by one of Chicago's own. In 1934, a truck transporting livestock rumbled past the Lincoln Tavern in downtown Chicago. One of the truck's passengers—a goat—fell off the back of the truck and wandered into the tavern. Proprietor and Cubs fan Billy Sianis adopted the visitor, named him Murphy, and soon changed the name of his establishment to the Billy Goat Tavern. The restaurant became a favorite spot for sports fans.

Years later, on October 6, 1945, the Cubs were hosting the Detroit Tigers in Game Four of the World Series, and "Billy Goat" Sianis purchased two tickets to the game: one for him and one for the goat. Alas, the goat was denied admission to Wrigley, and an irate Sianis declared, "The Cubs will never win a World Series so long as the goat is not allowed in Wrigley Field." After Sianis cast his hex, the Tigers won Game Four and, eventually, the series, and the curse was born. The Chicago Cubs have not played in a World Series since.

Chicago's collapse during the 1969 stretch run, when the team plummeted from nine games up to eight games back in a span of six weeks, is held up as a prime example of the goat's vengeance. Fifteen years later, the Cubs did invite a goat to opening day at Wrigley Field, and the team charged ahead to its first postseason berth in 39 years. Apparently the goat was not fully satisfied, however. After splitting the first four games of the best-of-five Championship Series with the San Diego Padres, the

*Billy Goat at the Billy Goat Tavern, 2003*

Cubs carried a 3-0 lead into the sixth inning of the fifth and deciding game, only to completely unravel. The league's Cy Young winner, Rick Sutcliffe, yielded six runs, aided by two costly errors by first baseman Leon Durham.

Bill Sianis' nephew Sam, and Sam's son Tom, brought a goat, allegedly a descendant of the original Murphy, to Wrigley Field before Game Six of the 2003 Championship Series. What transpired in that game would only feed the superstitions surrounding the power of the goat's curse. The team got within five outs of securing a trip to the World Series when a now-notorious spectator named Steve Bartman sparked a complete meltdown by the team. (The incident is discussed in further detail on the following pages.)

Despite attempts to break the curse by bringing various goats to Wrigley Field over the years, the curse continues to weigh heavily on fans and players. Boosters of opposing teams don't hesitate to invoke the goat legend to heckle Chicago, even on the Cubs' home turf. A St. Louis Cardinals fan holding a sign reading "The Curse Lives" and depicting images of a goat and Bartman got hosed down by Cubs pitcher Ryan Dempster before a game at Wrigley in 2006.

*Ryan Dempster hoses down a Cardinals fan's obnoxious sign, Wrigley Field, July 28, 2006*

*Sam (left) and Tom (right) Sianis and their goat companion, Wrigley Field, October 14, 2003*

# GAFFES AND CONTROVERSIES

Baseball is not an exact science. Human error plays a central role in the events on the field. The Chicago Cubs have been involved in two notorious examples of this.

In 1908, the Chicago Cubs were in a heated pennant race with the New York Giants and the Pittsburgh Pirates. The Cubs were in New York in late September for a four-game series at the Polo Grounds. They swept the opening doubleheader on September 22 to put themselves in a tie for first place with the Giants. On the 23rd, the game was tied 1-1 heading into the bottom of the ninth inning. New York had base runners on first and third with two outs when Al Bridwell singled to drive home Moose McCormick from third base with the apparent game-winning run. New York fans stormed the field in celebration. Meanwhile, 19-year-old Fred Merkle, the runner on first base, upon seeing McCormick cross the plate, left the base path without touching second base and headed for the clubhouse. Chicago's wily second baseman Johnny Evers noticed this and ran to retrieve the ball. (There is much debate as to whether or not he found the *actual* game ball.) Evers stepped on second base to force Merkle for the inning's third out, thus nullifying the run.

*Fred Merkle with the Cubs, 1918*

*Chicago Cubs vs. New York Giants, Polo Grounds, New York, October 8, 1908*

The umpire declared Merkle out, and the game remained tied. The fans could not be cleared from the field, however, and the teams had to schedule a make-up game for a later date. That date was October 8, and the Cubs won the game, 4-2, to finish the season in first place, one game ahead of the Giants and the Pirates. "Merkle's Boner," as the play came to be known in the baseball annals, is one of the game's more extraordinary moments, and it is Fred Merkle's main claim to fame. In an ironic twist, Merkle would later spend four seasons as Chicago's starting first baseman (1917–1920), and Bridwell was Chicago's shortstop in 1913.

Nearly a century later, the Cubs were on the flip side of a scenario in which the ill-conceived actions of one man ultimately led to the team's demise. In October of 2003, the Cubs were facing the Florida Marlins in the League Championship Series and playing for a chance to go to the World Series. Chicago won three of the first five games and needed to win just one of the last two to clinch the seven-game series. In Game Six at Wrigley, the Cubs mounted a 3-0 lead through seven innings and, after retiring the first batter in the eighth, were five outs away from their first Fall Classic since 1945. When Florida's Luis Castillo popped up into the left-field foul ground, it seemed as if the Cubs were about to get one out closer. Left fielder Moises Alou got under the ball—only to have fan Steve Bartman (along with several other, anonymous fans) reach up in an attempt to nab a souvenir. The ball bounced off Bartman's hands and was out of play. Alou was livid; the Cubs argued in vain for a call of fan interference; and the team imploded. Florida went on to score eight runs in the inning, thanks in no small part to a crucial error by shortstop Alex Gonzalez that might have been an inning-ending double play. Although Chicago briefly held a 5-3 advantage in Game Seven, Florida edged out a 9-6 win, and the Cubs once again went home disappointed. (The so-called Bartman Ball was blown up in February 2004 to help fans put the incident behind them.)

While the Giants of 1908 had every chance to win the make-up game despite Fred Merkle's gaffe, and the Cubs of 2003 could not blame Steve Bartman for Gonzalez's key error or their failure to secure Game Seven, the actions of those two men forever place them on the list of all-time sports goats.

*The "Bartman Ball" ready for explosion, February 26, 2004*

*Outfielder Moises Alou and fan Steve Bartman, October 14, 2003*

# HARD-LUCK PLAYERS

Success in baseball is never a sure thing. Players get hurt, move on to other teams, or simply fizzle out—and sometimes they meet even harsher fates. Every franchise has experienced the letdown of a young prospect coming up short of expectations, and the Cubs are no exception.

The shortstop on Chicago's 1918 pennant winner was a 22-year-old rookie named Charlie Hollocher. He led the team in hits, average, slugging, and stolen bases that year. In 1922, he batted .340 and struck out a mere five times in 592 at bats, still a franchise record. He was also an excellent defenseman. Hollocher hit a red-hot .342 in 1923 but played in only 66 games, taking a leave of absence due to depression. He attempted a comeback in 1924, still only 28 years old, but left halfway through the season and never played another game. His story ended tragically in 1940, when he committed suicide at the age of 44.

Another promising star who also met a sad fate just as his career was taking off was Eddie Waitkus. He signed with the Cubs in 1939, and after serving in the army, Waitkus emerged as a star in 1946. Two years later he was chosen for the All-Star Team. The Cubs traded Waitkus to Philadelphia after the 1948 season, and then the story turns dark. An overzealous fan from Chicago named Ruth Ann Steinhagen tracked Waitkus down at his hotel when the Phillies came to town to play the Cubs in June of 1949. Steinhagen shot Waitkus in the chest, nearly killing him. Although he continued playing until 1955, Waitkus was never the same. His story was the inspiration for the Roy Hobbs character in Bernard Malamud's *The Natural*.

One of baseball's saddest misfortunes was the loss of Ken Hubbs in the 1960s. The phenom second baseman won the National League's Rookie of the Year Award in 1962 and became the first rookie to win a Gold Glove. Early in 1964, Hubbs received a pilot's license in the hopes of conquering his fear of flying. In February, Hubbs was flying home to California from Utah. He hit bad weather and the plane went down, killing Hubbs and his passenger. Hubbs was 22 years old.

*Charlie Hollocher, 1918*

*Eddie Waitkus (right) with shortstop Lennie Merullo, 1941*

The Cubs have been spared such tragedies in recent years, but they have had their share of flops. Outfielder Jerome Walton won the Rookie of the Year Award while helping Chicago capture the East Division title in 1989, but he quickly fell into the ranks of "also-ran" and was out of baseball by 1998.

In 2001, the Cubs selected pitcher Mark Prior with the second overall pick in the amateur draft. He had a decent rookie campaign and then blossomed in his second year with a 18-6 record, 245 strikeouts, and a 2.43 ERA in 2003. Since then, Prior has been hampered by numerous injuries. He pitched in only nine games in 2006 and sat out the entire 2007 season following shoulder surgery. The young pitcher did not endear himself to fans, either, when he asked for an increase to his $3.65 million salary. It remains to be seen whether he lives up to his early promise, in a Cubs uniform or elsewhere.

*Ken Hubbs, Topps memorial baseball card, 1964*

*Mark Prior, 2003*

# THE OWNERS

The Chicago Cubs organization has had some illustrious names and great baseball minds at the top position within the club. Some owners inserted themselves directly into the daily operation of the team, while others were happy to take a backseat as the general managers and field managers used their expertise in pursuit of the ultimate goal: winning.

Grain and coal merchant William Hulbert was the team's principal owner and president from its inception until his death in 1882. He not only recruited top talent to Chicago, but he masterminded the formation of the National League in 1876. He helped to bring stability to the professional game and winning baseball to the city.

Hulbert's successor was no less notable an innovator. After one season as the team's star pitcher and two as manager, Albert Goodwill Spalding moved into the front office in 1878. He had received an ownership stake when Hulbert recruited him in

*Albert G. Spalding, 1890s*

1875, and following his boss's death in 1882, Spalding took over as president and principal owner. By this time, Spalding had also established his successful sporting goods business, which is where he was increasingly placing his attention. Spalding handed day-to-day control of the team to James Hart in 1892. Ten years later, Spalding sold all of his remaining ownership shares to Hart.

In 1905, the team was purchased by Charles Murphy, with the financial backing of Charles Taft. Murphy regularly butted heads with other owners, his managers, and his players, but it was under his watch that the franchise enjoyed its greatest dynasty. By 1914, Murphy was facing increasing hostility from other league owners, and he soon sold his stock to Taft.

The Cubs franchise was next taken in by Charles Weeghman, a Chicago restaurateur and owner of the Federal League's Chicago Whales franchise. When that league folded, Weeghman headed a group of investors to purchase the Cubs in 1916. He brought over some of his star Whales players and, perhaps most significantly, contributed the ballpark he had built for his previous club. Known at the time as Weeghman Park, the stadium would later be known as Wrigley Field.

Charles Weeghman's days at the helm did not last long. A series of financial stumbles forced him to sell off his shares to one of the club's other investors, chewing-gum magnate William Wrigley Jr., who assumed majority ownership of the franchise. Under Wrigley and team president William Veeck Sr., the ballpark was expanded and updated, games were broadcast on the radio, and the roster accumulated numerous star players. Wrigley passed away in 1932; Veeck died a year later.

After the senior Wrigley died, son Philip Knight "P. K." Wrigley ascended to the top spot. The younger Wrigley further expanded the media exposure on radio and, later, WGN-TV. He was an early proponent of using statistics and film to analyze player performance. P. K. also hired the son of his father's key advisor, Bill Veeck Jr. The younger Veeck, who was hired into the front office when he was just 20 years old, oversaw the planting of ivy on Wrigley Field's outfield walls.

Philip K. Wrigley died in 1977 at age 82, after 45 years as owner of the Chicago Cubs. His son, William Wrigley III, then took over. Four years later, in 1981, the Wrigleys sold the team

to the Tribune Company for $20.5 million—ending more than 60 years of ownership by the family.

In addition to winning, the Tribune Company was also interested in making money. One revolutionary change instituted by the Tribune was installing lights at Wrigley Field in 1988, thus ending a streak of more than 5,000 consecutive day games at the Friendly Confines. Andy McPhail, a third-generation baseball executive, ran the team for the Tribune as Cubs president and CEO beginning in 1994. He was replaced by John McDonough in 2006.

In April 2007, the Tribune Company was purchased by entrepreneur Sam Zell, and the new owner expressed his intention to sell off the Chicago Cubs after the 2007 season.

**Left:** *William Wrigley Jr. delivers ceremonial pitch at Wrigley Field, 1932*
**Below:** *Charles Murphy at West Side Grounds, 1913*

*Philip K. Wrigley (left) with player-manager Charlie Grimm and friend, 1934*

*Ed Lynch (left) and Andy McPhail (right), July 2000*

# GENERAL MANAGERS

The individuals who have been charged with running the Cubs' front-office operations have held various job titles and represent a range of personalities. Bill Veeck Sr., a former sportswriter, basically ran the Cubs from 1919 until his death in 1933. He made many of the key personnel decisions and helped to build a pennant-winning core. Veeck recruited the talents of Gabby Hartnett, Hack Wilson, Billy Herman, and others from the minor leagues and acquired Kiki Cuyler and Rogers Hornsby via trades to solidify a potent lineup. He also hired the then-unknown Joe McCarthy to manage the team in 1926.

Following Veeck, Phil Wrigley cycled through a handful of general managers—Charles "Boots" Weber, Jim Gallagher, and Wid Mathews—none of whom was able to establish a consistent winning tradition, and all of whom had to operate under Wrigley's close watch. Weber was at the helm for two pennants and six straight winning seasons but was fired after a sub-.500 campaign in 1940. Gallagher, another former newspaperman, served from 1940 to 1949 and was instrumental in establishing a farm system for player development, although the system was only marginally successful in producing talent for the parent club during his reign.

John Holland, who had been running the Cubs' Los Angeles Angels affiliate in the Pacific Coast League, had the longest tenure as the big league squad's GM (1957–1975). He helped to shape the strong rosters of the late 1960s through trades and the farm system, but he was also responsible for the greatest trading blunder in franchise history, when he sent Lou Brock to St. Louis. It was also during Holland's tenure that Chicago employed the ill-fated "College of Coaches" experiment in the early 1960s (see the "Managers" chapter).

Bob Kennedy, an alum of the College of Coaches, was hired as general manager in 1977 and was replaced by Herman Franks in May of 1981. Franks lasted until the end of the 1981 season, and during that five-month run, he endured a league-wide players' strike and the sale of the Cubs franchise.

Under the Tribune Company ownership, the Cubs had six general managers, none of whom held the job for more than six seasons. Dallas Green was hired away from the Philadelphia Phillies shortly after the Tribune took over, and he acquired several players from his former team, most notably the young Ryne Sandberg. Green helped to make the Cubs contenders in 1984 and earned the Executive of the Year Award. He also ruffled many feathers in the community, however, particularly for his push to have lights installed in storied Wrigley Field. He resigned in October 1987.

Jim Frey, the Cubs' field manager from 1984 to 1986, was hired to replace his old boss in December of 1987. Frey was active on the trading block, dealing closer Lee Smith and the popular Keith Moreland within the first few months on the job. In 1988, he swapped youngsters Rafael Palmeiro and Jamie Moyer for reliever Mitch Williams, who was a key cog for the 1989 division champions. After two sub-.500 seasons, Frey was fired in October 1991.

Former White Sox GM Larry Himes was hired the same day that Frey was fired. Himes practically stole Sammy Sosa from his old team before the 1992 season, but he also let top talent like Greg Maddux, Rick Sutcliffe, and Andre Dawson walk away as free agents. He also hastened the early (but temporary) retirement of Sandberg in 1994, which proved to be Himes' last year on the job.

Under Ed Lynch's five-year term as general manager, the Cubs posted only one winning season (1998), and in July of 2000, Andy MacPhail, the president and CEO, assumed Lynch's duties and continued to do so for two years. In July 2002, MacPhail promoted assistant GM Jim Hendry to be the new general manager. The team has had many ups and downs under Hendry, but the acquisition of Aramis Ramirez, Derrek Lee, Alfonso Soriano, Ted Lilly, and others through trades and free agency have helped to make Chicago a contender again. The Cubs invested more than $300 million during the 2007 offseason to sign players and hire new manager Lou Piniella.

*William Wrigley Jr. (left) with Joe McCarthy (center) and Bill Veeck Sr. (right), 1926*

*Jim Gallagher (left) with Philip K. Wrigley (center) and Bill Veeck Jr. (right), 1940*

*Jim Hendry with manager Lou Piniella at spring training, February 2007*

*Jim Hendry with newly signed Alfonso Soriano, November 2006*

# TRADING-BLOCK BRILLIANCE AND BLUNDERS

The Cubs front office has shown flashes of brilliance over the years by finagling some dazzling ballplayers into a Cubs uniform. Other times, the management has left fans shaking their heads with foolhardy moves that spelled prolonged agony for the club.

William Hulbert's maneuver to acquire four stars from the Boston club during the National Association's 1875 season may have been contrary to the rules and spirit of the league, but there's no denying that it helped to create a winner in Chicago. Similarly, when James Hart sent pitcher Jack Taylor and catcher Larry McLean to St. Louis in exchange for Mordecai "Three Finger" Brown, he brought in a cornerstone of a dynasty—not to mention a future Hall of Famer and the best pitcher in franchise history.

Late in 1917, Philadelphia Phillies owner Bill Baker accepted Mike Prendergast and "Pickles" Dillhoefer, along with $55,000 in cash, from the Cubs in exchange for Grover Cleveland "Pete" Alexander and Bill Killefer. Alexander, already one of the league's best hurlers, went on to win more than 120 games for Chicago on a fast track to Cooperstown. Later in the same month of December 1917, however, the Cubs returned the favor by shipping Cy Williams to Philadelphia for Dode Paskert. Not yet 30 years old, Williams unleashed a decade of strong seasons for the Phillies, while the aging Paskert stuck around Chicago for three mediocre years.

No discussion about bad trades, by any franchise, can ignore the colossal gaffe that Chicago committed on June 15, 1964, when outfielder Lou Brock was shipped to the Cubs' biggest rival, the St. Louis Cardinals, for three unremarkable players. The biggest return on the deal for Chicago was a 7-19 record over three years from pitcher Ernie Broglio. St. Louis, meanwhile, went on to win the World Series in 1964 and 1967 and a pennant in 1968 with Brock. The six-time All-Star set stolen base records and piled up a mountain of hits. His 3,000th career hit came against his former team, in August 1979. Faithful fans can only imagine how the Cubs might have fared had they had the speedster Brock leading off with Billy Williams, Ron Santo, and Ernie Banks hitting behind him.

Partial redemption came in 1966 when Chicago acquired Ferguson Jenkins from Philadelphia for Larry Jackson and Bob Buhl. Jackson and Buhl had been two of Chicago's top starters, but their careers were all but done. Jenkins, meanwhile, reeled off six consecutive 20-win seasons with the Cubs en route to the Hall of Fame.

The heart and soul of the Cubs in the 1980s and 1990s was acquired in one of the franchise's all-time steals. In 1982, Chicago sent shortstop Ivan DeJesus to Philadelphia for veteran Larry Bowa and infield prospect Ryne Sandberg. "Ryno" went on to become a legend of the game, piling up records and securing his place in the hearts of Cubs fans everywhere. The Sandberg deal also helped fans forget that just two years earlier they had sent Bruce Sutter to the Cardinals for Leon Durham, Ken Reitz, and Ty Waller. Durham served Chicago well in seven-plus seasons, but Sutter was baseball's top relief pitcher and the closer on St. Louis' 1982 championship team.

Sammy Sosa came to the Cubs on March 30, 1992, in a deal that sent George Bell to the White Sox. Bell had been a one-season star with the Cubs, but he was out of baseball after the 1993 season. Within days of his arrival, Sosa was getting tips from legendary Cubs hitter Billy Williams at spring training, and he went on to help rejuvenate the city, and major league baseball, with his home run prowess in the late 1990s and early 2000s.

*Charles Weeghman (right) shaking hands with newly acquired Pete Alexander, 1917*

*Dode Paskert, 1918*

*Lou Brock at spring training, 1963*

*Sammy Sosa (left) with coach Billy Williams at spring training, April 1992*

*Cap Anson*

*Frank Chance at the 1910 World Series*

# MANAGERS

As owners and general managers work behind the scenes to assemble the pieces to build a winner, it falls to the managers to get results on the field. Through 2007, 56 different men have skippered the Cubs, ranging from fill-ins like Roy Johnson, Joe Altobelli, and Rene Lachemann—each of whom managed (and lost) one game for Chicago—to long-timers like Cap Anson, who manned the helm for more than 2,200 games, and Charlie Grimm, who took three turns as chief between 1932 and 1960.

Adrian "Cap" Anson came to Chicago as a 24-year-old first baseman in 1876, and within three years he had the managerial reins as well, which he held for 19 seasons. In the course of amassing a record of 1,283 wins and 932 losses, Anson guided the team to five league titles. His win and loss totals as manager remain franchise records more than a century later.

Anson was a tough act to follow, and after three relative short-timers, another first baseman led the way starting in 1905. Frank Chance took over where his predecessor, Frank Selee, left off in building a winner in the Windy City. When Selee contracted tuberculosis and retired early in 1905, Chance assumed a player-manager role. The Peerless Leader captained the team to three straight pennants and a winning percentage of .664 in seven and a half seasons. He is the only player-manager ever to win two World Series—and in Game Three of the 1910 series he earned the distinction of being the first player ejected from a World Series tilt. While Anson frowned on players drinking

*Rogers Hornsby (center) with Cubs players at spring training, 1931*

*Charlie Grimm (center) with Cubs players, mid-1930s*

and carousing, Chance had no problem joining his boys for a few cocktails after a game—all in the name of team morale, of course.

Joe McCarthy was a 39-year-old minor league manager with no major league experience when Bill Veeck Sr. hired him to pilot the Cubs in 1926. McCarthy's crew pulled together five straight winning years, and a trip to the 1929 Series, before he departed with four days left in the 1930 season. (He moved on to command a legendary dynasty with the New York Yankees.)

Second baseman Rogers Hornsby was named McCarthy's successor. Undoubtedly one of the best ballplayers of the twentieth century, he was also among the surliest, a quality that made his transition to manager a rocky one. Photographer George Brace, who covered the Cubs for many years, observed that Hornsby's "big problem was that he expected everyone to be as good as him. The players hated him." By August of 1932, the players had had enough of Hornsby's gruffness, and first baseman Charlie Grimm assumed player-manager duties.

In stark contrast to Hornsby, Grimm was a jovial chap who got along well with just about everyone. "Jolly Cholly" started as a major leaguer at the age of 17 and had been Chicago's first baseman since 1925. His cool head was a welcome reprieve. The players responded by closing out the 1932 season with a 37-18 record under Grimm—including a 14-game winning streak in August—and capturing another league crown. Grimm ceded first base to Phil Cavarretta in 1935, and the team charged ahead to another pennant. Midway through 1938, Grimm left the dugout and headed to the broadcast booth, handing the reins to his star catcher, Gabby Hartnett, who carried the team the rest of the way to the World Series.

Charlie Grimm was back for another go as manager in 1944, and other than a surprising NL title in 1945, his second term was not as successful as the first. In 1949, owner P. K. Wrigley shifted Grimm from field manager to the front office. A virtual managerial carousel followed, including stints by star players Cavarretta and Stan Hack and the return of Grimm for 17 games in 1960. Cavarretta's ultimate downfall was his honesty. When asked during spring training in 1954 what he thought of the team's chances, Cavarretta replied that they didn't have the talent to contend. He became one of the few managers to be fired at spring training. The Cubs ended the 1954 season, with Hack as manager, in seventh place, 33 games out of first.

Frustrated by the inability to find a manager that suited his tastes, Wrigley resolved to institute an innovative, and ultimately flawed, system known as the College of Coaches, beginning in 1961. Under that strategy, four coaches would rotate into the "head coach" position during the season (plus another four in the minor leagues), each imparting his own wisdom to the players. In reality, the system generated chaos and confusion, with a different set of rules and leadership styles coming into play depending on the manager of the day. The result was a 64-90 record and another seventh-place finish. It was even worse in 1962. Despite a lineup that included Ernie Banks, Billy Williams, Ron Santo, Lou Brock, and Ken Hubbs, the team mounted a franchise-worst 59-103 record under the College of Coaches.

Leo Durocher was brought in before the 1966 season, and abrasive and cantankerous as he was, he brought stability and demanded the best from his players. After a disastrous first year on the job, Durocher was able to harness the roster's talent and lead it back to winning ways. But his old-school, authoritarian style did not always mesh well with the modern athlete, and "Leo the Lip" was frequently at odds with his players. He was fired midway through the 1972 season. Following the luckless 1966 campaign, the Cubs won 53 percent of their games under Durocher. He is one of only four men to manage 1,000 games for Chicago.

Following Durocher, the club went through 11 managers in 15 years before settling on someone who was able to hold the job for as long as three complete seasons. Don Zimmer had the helm from 1988 to 1991 and guided the Cubs to the 1989 National League East crown; he won the 1989 Manager of the Year Award.

After taking the San Francisco Giants to the 2002 World Series, Dusty Baker walked away to manage Chicago in 2003.

*Leo Durocher, early in the 1966 season*

He proceeded to lead the team to its first division title in 14 years and within five outs of the World Series. They barely missed the playoffs in 2004, and the team slipped to sixth place by 2006, which proved to be Baker's last turn with the team.

The fiery Lou Piniella was hired before the 2007 season. With two decades of managerial experience under his belt, including a World Series championship, Piniella helped to re-energize the Chicago Cubs and carry them to a division title.

**Right:** *Don Zimmer gives the umpire an earful during a Cubs-Mets game, April 24, 1989*

*Lou Piniella argues a call at Wrigley Field, June 2, 2007*

# PLAYER SALARIES

Ross Barnes' performance in 1876 was most impressive. He led the league in average, hits, runs, doubles, triples, and walks, and finished among the top five in just about every other category. The following season, Chicago owed him a $2,500 salary. A long illness affected his performance in 1877, however, and the club decided to deduct $1,000 from his pay. Barnes griped about the decision, but could do little about it. One hundred and thirty years later, Derrek Lee is due to be paid $13,250,000 by the Cubs—and not a nickel will be deducted without considerable legal wrangling between Lee's agents and the Cubs organization.

The professional baseball salaries of today are simply unimaginable in the context of the sport's early years. For the first one hundred years of major league baseball, the balance of power was wholly in the hands of the team owners. The reserve clause, first implemented in 1879, was part of all player contracts and stated that, in effect, the rights to a player were held by the team in perpetuity; even after a contract expired, the player could sign with another team only if his current team let him. The one tool that players had in their arsenal to try to force an owner's hand was the holdout, or simply refusing to show up to play.

After a disappointing outing with Chicago in 1939, former All-Star pitcher Dizzy Dean was offered a 50-percent pay cut for the 1940 season. Dean, who acknowledged that the value of his right arm had declined, was hoping for $15,000 but ultimately relented to Chicago's $10,000 offer. (The 30-year-old pitcher saw only limited action for the 1940 Cubs.)

Still, many professional ballplayers were able to enjoy the good life. Center fielder Augie Galan showed off a sleek new Lincoln Zephyr not long after he put together an all-star season in 1936.

The reserve clause was finally eliminated in 1975, opening the door to the free-agent era and sky-high salaries. Rick Sutcliffe signed with Chicago as a free agent after the 1984 season and became the franchise's first million-dollar man ($1.26 million, to be exact). By 1989, his annual salary topped $2.3 million, third most in the National League. Sutcliffe and Andre Dawson were the only Cubs to earn over a million dollars for the 1989 division champs. Two years later, Dawson became Chicago's first three-million-dollar man, raking in $3,325,000. Greg Maddux followed as the highest-paid Cub with a $4.2 million payday for 1992, and Ryne Sandberg flirted with six million in 1993, enjoying a $5.975 million income. Sammy Sosa's home run explosion in the late 1990s also led to a paycheck explosion. After making a "mere" $5.5 million in 1997, Sosa signed a four-year contract extension in 2001 that had him earning $16 million by 2004. In August of 2007, Carlos Zambrano signed a five-year deal worth $91.5 million, plus bonuses and an option for a sixth year at $19.25 million.

Eighteen players on the Cubs' 2007 squad earned more than a million dollars, and three of them—Zambrano, Lee, and Alfonso Soriano—were in the eight-digit realm. Add to that product endorsements and other revenue streams, and a star players' income today is simply off the charts.

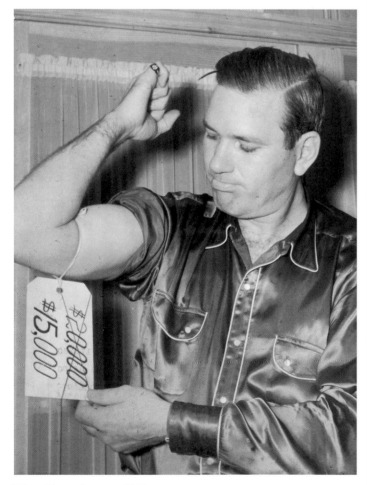

*Dizzy Dean, January 1940*

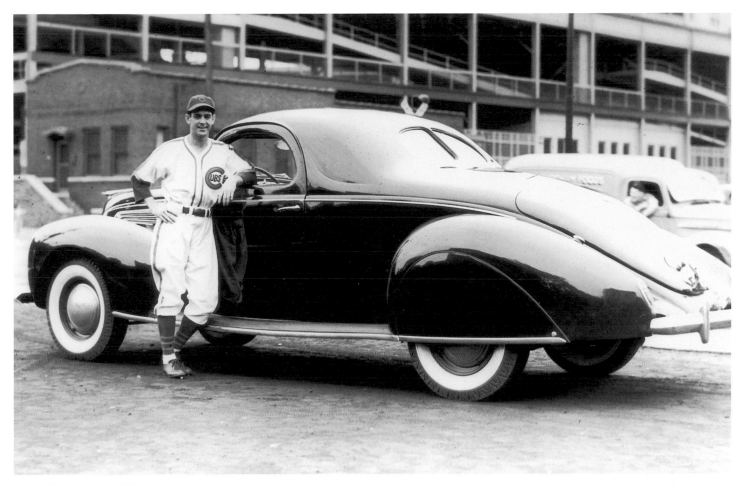

*Augie Galan, circa 1938*

*Sammy Sosa, with his wife, Sonia, and son, Sammy Jr., after signing his contract extension, March 16, 2001*

*Carlos Zambrano with general manager Jim Hendry, August 17, 2007*

# THE RACE BARRIER

For nearly a hundred years, African Americans were excluded from all ranks of major league baseball. While there was no formal rule excluding blacks, a strict gentlemen's agreement among league owners did just that. Cap Anson was instrumental in fostering segregation in the sport. In July 1887 he refused to allow his White Stockings to play an exhibition game against the International League's Newark Little Giants if African-American pitcher George Stovey and catcher Moses "Fleet" Walker took the field. Anson's decision sparked the International League to suspend the signing of any more black players. The National League soon followed suit with an unofficial ban on black players. Although Anson, a notorious racist, is often held to blame for baseball's long-standing color barrier, generations of owners and executives maintained the status quo for another 60 years.

With no welcome access to the majors, black players organized their own teams and leagues. The Chicago area hosted several premier black teams in the early 1900s. The Leland Giants featured a star pitcher named Rube Foster, and although record-keeping was spotty, the team was rumored to post a record of 110 wins and 10 losses in 1907, followed by an even more impressive 126-6 record in 1910. Foster gained control of the team in 1910 and renamed it the Chicago American Giants. Known as "the father of black baseball," Foster formed the Negro National League in 1920, providing a structured season for teams around the nation. Foster's Giants won five Negro National League titles, including the first three from 1920 to 1922. The league folded in 1931, and the American Giants later joined subsequent leagues, including a second Negro National League (1933–1935) and the Negro American League (1937–1950).

When Jackie Robinson broke major league baseball's color barrier in 1947, he paved the way for countless more to follow. It took the Chicago Cubs six more years to integrate. In September 1953, the team called up Gene Baker and Ernie Banks from the minors. Banks, who had spent three seasons with the Kansas City Monarchs of the Negro American League, made his major league debut on September 17. The 22-year-old infielder kicked off his Hall of Fame career by going 0-for-3 with an error. Despite the

*1905 Leland Giants*

*1922 Chicago American Giants*

high racial tension in Chicago and the rest of the nation during the 1950s and 1960s, Banks quickly won over the fans, white and black alike, not simply for his athletic abilities, but also his dedication to and enthusiasm for the game.

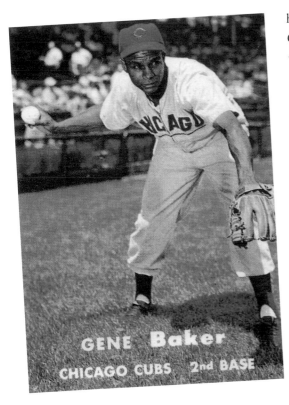

*Gene Baker, Topps baseball card, 1957*

Gene Baker, six years Banks' senior, made his on-field debut three days after Banks, as a pinch hitter. He had been a standout in the Cubs farm system since 1950 and prior to that had starred with the Monarchs. Some charged Philip Wrigley and the Cubs with racism for being so slow to call up Baker at a time when the team was desperate for talent. Originally a shortstop, Baker shifted to second base to make room for Banks. By 1954 he was the team's regular pivot man, playing alongside Banks in major league baseball's first all-black double-play combination.

As more and more black players joined the majors in the 1950s, they remained shut out from coaching and managerial positions. In 1962, the Cubs broke the barrier on the coaching front by hiring Buck O'Neil. A former Negro Leagues star, O'Neil had managed the Monarchs for seven seasons before the Cubs hired him in 1956 as a scout and instructor in their minor league system. He coached for Chicago until 1965 and then returned to a scouting role with the club for nearly two decades.

To the posthumous chagrin of Cap Anson, the twenty-first-century Cubs hired two African Americans to lead the team on the field. Before the 2000 season, Don Baylor was hired as Chicago's first black skipper, a position he held for nearly three full seasons. Dusty Baker ascended to the top post in 2003 and led the team to its first division crown in 14 seasons in his first year with the Cubs.

*Ernie Banks, 1953*

*Don Baylor, November 1, 1999*

# CUBS ROOTS

The Windy City has long been a rich melting pot of ethnicities, nationalities, and races. Some of that legacy is represented in the men who have worn the Cubs uniform. The city's proud Irish community cheered on the great Mike "King" Kelly during the 1880s, and in the 1910s, Dublin-born Jimmy Archer starred as Chicago's starting catcher.

Up through the 1950s, ball clubs throughout the majors were composed almost exclusively of white, American-born players. Latin Americans occasionally appeared on rosters during the first half of the twentieth century. Hiram Bithorn, the first Puerto Rican in the big leagues, pitched for Chicago in the 1940s. He debuted in 1942 and in 1943 led the club with 18 wins and a 2.60 ERA. He served in the Navy during World War II and then played one more season before retiring in 1947, at the age of 31. He died in mysterious circumstances in 1951, allegedly shot by a Mexican policeman. The main baseball stadium in San Juan, Puerto Rico, is named in Bithorn's honor.

The end of baseball's ban against black players in the late 1940s opened the door to larger numbers of Latin Americans as well. Following the trail blazed by Bithorn, numerous Latinos have starred with the Cubs. Cuban-born Jose Cardenal roamed the Chicago outfield from 1972 to 1976 and twice batted above .300.

*Hi Bithorn, 1946*

*Jimmy Archer, 1913*

Manny Trillo, from Venezuela, joined the team in 1975 and held down the second base position for four seasons; he returned to Chicago for the twilight of his career in the late 1980s. In 1977, Trillo was joined in the infield by Puerto Rican shortstop Ivan DeJesus. With Cardenal and Jerry Morales, another Puerto Rican, in the outfield, Chicago's had four regular starters of Latin American descent on its 1977 roster.

The arrival of Sammy Sosa in the 1990s electrified the Latino community in Chicago and around the nation. Hailing from the "baseball factory" of the Dominican Republic, Sosa is one of more than 400 Dominicans to have played in the majors since the 1950s. Outfielder Henry Rodriguez (Dominican Republic) and third baseman Jose Hernandez (Puerto Rico) started alongside Sosa on the 1998 Wild Card team, and Geremi Gonzalez (Venezuela) started 20 games as a pitcher, among other Latino utility players and spot starters.

Hee Seop Choi brought an eastern influence to the team in 2002. The South Korean native played two mediocre seasons at first base before being traded to Florida for Derrek Lee.

Chicago's 2007 roster looks decidedly different from its 1907 version, demographically. Today's Cubs are a diverse group, with ten foreign-born players on the active roster, including four Dominicans, three Venezuelans, one Puerto Rican, a German, and a Canadian. Aramis Ramirez, from Santo Domingo in the Dominican Republic, has been the team's top hitter since he arrived in Chicago in 2004, and no Cub has won more games on the mound than Venezuelan Carlos Zambrano since 2001. Their closer, Ryan Dempster, was born in Canada.

*Jose Cardenal, 1977*

*Hee Seop Choi, 2003*

*Carlos Zambrano and Aramis Ramirez, 2004*

*Johnny Kling, 1907*

# CATCHERS

Chicago's backstops have long been integral to the club's success on the field. The powerhouse teams of the early 1900s featured an outstanding defensive catcher who was also dangerous with the bat. Johnny Kling was the main starter behind the plate from 1901 to 1908. He left in 1909 after winning a billiard tournament, hoping to make a go at a new career, but it didn't last, and he was back with the Cubs in 1910. In his prime, Kling led National League catchers in fielding percentage four times, and during the 1907 World Series he threw out seven Detroit base runners, denying the legendary Ty Cobb a stolen base.

Versatility behind the plate and at the plate was one of the great assets of Gabby Hartnett. The son of an accomplished semi-pro catcher, Hartnett turned in league-leading stats among catchers, providing high averages (.297 lifetime), solid RBI numbers (including a career-best 122 in 1930), a healthy supply of home runs (236 in his career), and excellent defense. A 19-year

veteran with the Cubs, Hartnett was a vital part of four World Series teams (1929, 1932, 1935, 1938), and he won the league MVP in 1935. Hartnett became player-manager in 1938 and helped to secure the pennant with his famous "Homer in the Gloamin'." In the midst of a heated pennant race, the Cubs and Pirates were tied 5-5 in a game at Wrigley on September 28. As darkness and haze settled in the skies above Chicago, Hartnett drove a two-strike, two-out pitch into the seats in the bottom of the ninth inning. The win catapulted the Cubs ahead of Pittsburgh into first place, capping off an impressive late-season surge. Chicago clinched the pennant three days later. Hartnett continued to serve as manager while catching part-time through 1940. After he played out his final year, as a New York Giant in 1941, Hartnett's bat and catcher's mask were sent to the National Baseball Hall of Fame, where Hartnett was himself inducted in 1955.

It would have been difficult for anyone to fill Gabby Hartnett's shin guards, but the arrival of Randy Hundley a quarter of a century later added a much-needed piece to a team on the rise. Hundley hit 19 homers and drove in 63 runs as a rookie in 1966 and led all NL catchers with 85 assists. He was a workhorse who never wanted to sit out, and in 1968, he appeared in 160 games. A Gold Glove winner in 1967, Hundley recorded a .992 fielding percentage through his first four full seasons before injuries slowed him down.

The next long-term presence behind the plate was Jody Davis, who joined Chicago in 1981 and became the full-time starter in his second season. Davis was stellar during the 1984 League Championship Series, and in 1986, he won a Gold Glove Award while also leading the Cubs with 21 homers. Very popular with the fans, he was a rock at the backstop position, catching at least 138 games in every season from 1983 to 1986. Davis rejoined the Cubs system as a minor league manager in 2006.

The Cubs had five catchers who logged at least 100 innings behind the plate in 2007. Michael Barrett had been the primary starter since 2004, but a dugout tussle with pitcher Carlos Zambrano expedited his departure in mid-2007. Veterans Jason Kendall and Henry Blanco stepped in, until the young Geovany Soto assumed most of the burden late in the season. The rugged, 230-pound Soto batted .389 and slugged .667 in 18 games in 2007.

*Gabby Hartnett, 1932*

*Geovany Soto tagging out Cincinnati's Norris Hopper, 2007*

# First Basemen

Probably no position in franchise history is stacked with more talent than first base—from Hall of Famers Cap Anson and Frank Chance to "Mr. Cub" himself, Ernie Banks, to the beloved Mark "Amazing" Grace and now All-Star Derrek Lee. Throw in Charlie Grimm, Phil Cavarretta, and the oft-maligned Bill Buckner, and you have a virtual all-star team of first basemen.

When William Hulbert wrested Cap Anson from the rival Philadelphia ballclub in 1875, he acquired one of the dominant players of the nineteenth century and a Chicago mainstay for more than two decades. (Anson's accomplishments are discussed in more detail in the following chapter, "Hit Men.")

Frank Chance arrived in Chicago in 1898, a year after Anson departed. He was discovered in California's semipro leagues and spent most of his first seasons in the majors as a catcher and outfielder. In 1902, he shifted to first base and earned a full-time job there the following year. The move suited him well. He batted a career-high .327 in 1903, drove in 81 runs, and led the league with 67 stolen bases. Chance went on to pilfer 400 bases in his career and remains the franchise record holder, a rare role for a first baseman. He was a tough player who took nearly 150 lumps from pitchers in his career; he also holds the franchise mark for times hit by pitch. During Chicago's impressive 1906 season, the Peerless Leader batted .319 and led the

league in stolen bases (57) and runs scored (103), while also serving as manager. In four World Series appearances, Chance batted .300, including a stellar .421 in 1908. An imposing presence on the field, Chance became one of the most effective defensive first basemen in the league and, of course, the anchor of the Tinker-to-Evers-to-Chance double-play threat. The combination of solid hitting, great speed, superior fielding, and strong leadership led to Chance's induction into the Baseball Hall of Fame in 1946.

Chicago's next longtime first baseman arrived in 1925, just as the team was building a talented core. After five seasons in Pittsburgh, Charlie Grimm arrived in Chicago and took over first base. He batted .306 and led the team with 76 RBI that year. His nine seasons as the starting first baseman were marked by consistency and solid play. He batted over .300 four times and was a tough guy to strike out.

Grimm handed the first-base mantle to 18-year-old Phil Cavarretta in 1935. Originally signed as a pitcher, Cavarretta quickly showed his hitting prowess in the minor leagues. He homered in his first start with the big league club in 1934 and then stuck with Chicago for the next 20 seasons, spending time in the outfield as well as first base. His first of four straight All-Star seasons came in 1944, when he batted .321 and collected 197 hits. "Philliabuck," as he was called, took it up a notch for the pennant run in 1945, winning the batting title (.355) and the league MVP Award. A clutch performer, Cavarretta batted .462 and .423 in the 1938 and 1945 World Series, respectively. He still ranks among the franchise career leaders in games, at bats, runs, hits, triples, runs batted in, and walks. Known as a hustle player, Cavarretta was adored by fans and teammates. He was named player-manager midway through the 1951 season and held the spot until 1953. He played out his final two seasons across town with the White Sox before retiring in 1955.

In 1962, the Cubs shifted a true legend from shortstop to first base. Ernie Banks played more games at first (1,259) than he did at short (1,125), but shortstop is where he first established his Hall of Fame credentials—and his accomplishments are detailed in the shortstops chapter of this book.

When Chicago received Bill Buckner from Los Angeles in an offseason trade in 1977, it acquired a pure contact hitter who

*Cap Anson, playing first base*

Charlie Grimm

Frank Chance, rounding third base, at West Side Grounds

Phil Cavarretta, 1945

rarely struck out and batted over .300 four times in seven seasons with the Cubs, including a batting crown in 1980. Buckner was used primarily in the outfield while with the Dodgers but was converted to full-time first baseman in Chicago—much to the relief of Buckner and his gimpy ankles.

A standout player at San Diego State University, Mark Grace made his major league debut in 1988 and remained the Cubs' first baseman for 13 seasons. Grace possessed only average power for the position but more than made up for it with high batting averages and stingy defense. He was a four-time Gold Glove Award winner, holds the NL single-season record for assists by a first baseman, and regularly finished among the league leaders in hits, batting average, on base percentage, doubles, and walks. Like Buckner, Grace rarely struck out, and the respect that pitchers had for him is evidenced by the frequency with which he received free passes, including a career-high 14 intentional walks in 1993. He piled up nearly 2,500 hits (2,201 with Chicago) and more than 500 doubles in his 16-year career, and he was a lifetime .308 hitter as a Cub. Grace is arguably the best fielding first baseman the Cubs have ever had, and he surely ranks among the franchise's all-time legends. Of course, it was only after he left Chicago to sign with the Arizona Diamondbacks, in 2001, that Grace was able to add a World Series championship ring to his collection.

Chicago's latest force at first base is amassing legendary numbers of his own. Traded from the Florida Marlins before the 2004 season, Derrek Lee was one of four Cubs to belt at least 30 homers that year. He followed that with a league-best .335 average in 2005, along with career highs in home runs (46), RBI (107), runs (120), hits (199), doubles (50), slugging (.662), and on base percentage (.418). He was voted to the All-Star Game and won a Gold Glove—all of which landed him third place in the MVP voting for 2005. After missing most of 2006 due to injury, he rebounded in 2007 with 22 homers and a .317 average, as well as another All-Star appearance. Lee signed a five-year contract extension before the 2006 season, ensuring that he will be one to watch at Wrigley for years to come.

*Bill Buckner, 1981*

*Mark Grace, 1998*

*Derrek Lee, 2007*

# Hit Men

Through baseball's long history there have been players who were a threat to get on base every time they stepped to the plate. Cap Anson was just such a player. The 2,995 hits he collected while wearing a Chicago uniform between 1876 and 1897 remain a franchise record. He was the first player to amass 3,000 hits in a career (including his time with Philadelphia and Rockford in the National Association), and his 3,418 lifetime total was unchallenged until Ty Cobb passed him, nearly a quarter-century after Anson retired. Though he won only two batting titles, Anson's average topped .300 nineteen times, with a high of .399 in 1881. As an ad for Young Sports' Publication proclaimed, Anson—"King of the Diamond, Prince of Batters"—was also a force at billiards, pigeon shooting, and even cricket. The Hall of Famer was first exposed to baseball while serving as a drummer boy in the Civil War.

The late 1920s and 1930s saw an explosion in offensive production around the league, and the Cubs featured several players who made the most of the hitter-friendly era. Kiki Cuyler, Rogers Hornsby, Riggs Stephenson, and Hack Wilson all batted .345 or higher in 1929, and Hornsby set a franchise-record with 229 base hits. Cuyler came one short a year later with 228 hits, one of three Cubs to break the 200-hit plateau in 1930. Second baseman Billy Herman collected more than 200 hits in a season three times from 1932 to 1936. Stan Hack joined the hit parade later in the decade; the 2,193 hits he collected during

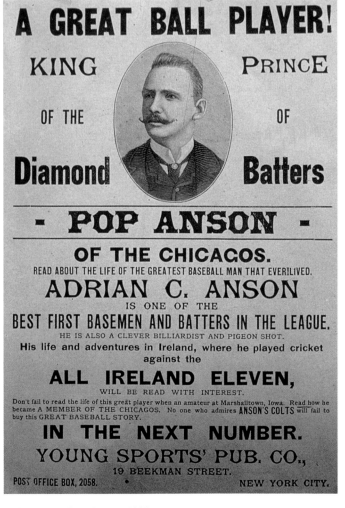

*Ad featuring Cap Anson, 1880s*

*Louisville Slugger ad featuring Kiki Cuyler, Rogers Hornsby, Hack Wilson, Charlie Grimm, and Riggs Stephenson, 1929*

his 16-year career, all with Chicago, rank him sixth on the all-time franchise list.

The incomparable Ernie Banks spent his entire career as a Cub as well, and his 2,583 hits are second only to Anson's total. Banks' longtime teammate and fellow Hall of Famer, Billy Williams, is not far behind, with 2,510. Arguably the best left-handed hitter in franchise history, Williams had three 200-hit seasons, and he won a batting title in 1972.

Fans of more recent Cubs ball were treated to a trio of hit men in the 1980s and 1990s. Although his only 200-hit outing came in 1984 when he was in just his third year, Ryne Sandberg collected at least 150 hits in 11 consecutive seasons and ranks fourth on the all-time franchise list. During his prime, Sandberg often had guys like Andre Dawson (2,774 career hits) and Mark Grace hitting behind him in the lineup. The left-handed Grace collected more hits than any other major leaguer during the 1990s; not counting the strike-shortened 1994 season, he averaged 182 hits for the decade.

Although he is mostly remembered for hitting balls over the fence, Sammy Sosa accumulated all sorts of base hits during his monumental run from 1998 to 2001. He averaged an even 190 hits and a .310 average during that four-year run. In 2006, center fielder Juan Pierre became the first Cub since Sandberg to collect 200 hits in a season.

*Mark Grace, 1999*

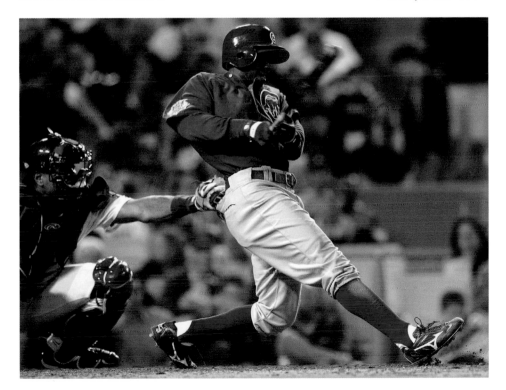

*Juan Pierre, 2006*

# SECOND BASEMEN

O ne of Chicago's legendary greats, Ryne Sandberg, manned the second base position for 15 seasons. More than a century earlier, the team had its first star at the position. In the inaugural season of the National League, Ross Barnes posted a league-best—and all-time franchise record—batting average of .429. He was also tops in the league in on base percentage, slugging percentage, hits, runs, doubles, triples, and walks, and second in runs batted in. Barnes proved to be a one-hit wonder for the White Stockings, however, and moved on after a sub-par 1877.

The five-foot-nine-inch-tall, 125-pound Johnny Evers was a combative, aggressive competitor. He's best known for being the pivot man in the team's fabled double-play combo of the early

*Ross Barnes, 1870s*

*Johnny Evers, 1910*

1900s. A career .270 hitter, Evers thrived in October, batting .350 in Chicago's World Series victories in 1907 and 1908. His best regular-season production came in 1912, when he hit .341. Evers was also an aggressive base runner and stole a career-best 49 bases in 1906.

Although Rogers Hornsby's best years were behind him by the time he arrived in Chicago in 1929 at the age of 33, his accomplishments that season rank among the best ever by a Cubs player: 229 hits, 156 runs, 47 doubles, 39 home runs, 149 RBI, .380 batting average, and .679 slugging percentage. The MVP performance helped carry the team to the pennant. Hornsby would later remark that the 1929 Cubs had "the best individual talent of any team I ever played on." He was a fiercely confident man, and his irritable moods did not always sit well with teammates. Hornsby moved into a player-manager role at the tail end of the 1930 season, and he put up decent numbers as a player in 1931. By early 1932, however,

"Rajah" had worn out his welcome, as both player and manager, in Chicago.

The man for whom Hornsby benched himself was Billy Herman, who debuted late in 1931. In his first full season of 1932, Herman batted .314 and collected 206 hits, leading the team in both categories. He was one of the best fielding second basemen of his era. As a 22-year-old rookie, he led all NL second baseman in assists and fielding chances, and in 1933 he set the National League record for putouts in a season (466), which still stands. His best offensive output was in 1935, when he played in all 154 games and posted career marks in average (.341), hits (227), runs (113), and doubles (57). Though difficult to measure statistically, he was also viewed by many as the best hit-and-run man in the game as well as a great bunter. Herman started off the 1941 season slowly, and the Cubs traded him to Brooklyn, where he continued his Hall of Fame career. He made 10 consecutive All-Star appearances from 1934 to 1943.

*Rogers Hornsby, 1929*

*Billy Herman, 1930s*

Chicago had great hopes for another star second baseman when Ken Hubbs came on the scene in 1962 and won the Rookie of the Year Award. A fan favorite, the young Hubbs set fielding records in his first season. Tragically, he died in a plane crash after the 1963 season. The hole was filled admirably by Glenn Beckert, who had been a shortstop in the minors but shifted over after Hubbs' death. A decent hitter—he batted .283 in nine seasons with the Cubs—Beckert rarely struck out. The four-time All-Star was paired with shortstop Don Kessinger in a formidable double-play combo for nearly a decade.

It is a close race for all-time fan favorite between Ernie Banks and Ryne Sandberg. Like Banks, Ryno's popularity extended beyond the Wrigley Field bleachers to baseball fans all over the country. He had been a multi-sport star in high school but eventually focused on baseball. When he arrived in Chicago in 1982, Sandberg played third base and hit .271, stole 32 bases, and scored 103 runs as a rookie. He moved to second base in 1983, and by 1984, at the age of 24, he was a veritable star. Sandberg's consistent play and rare combination of power, speed, and defense helped him garner the National League MVP Award in 1984, nine consecutive Gold Gloves (a record streak for his position), and ten straight All-Star selections. He scored 100 or more runs in seven seasons and drove in that many twice. His 282 career home runs were the most by a second baseman when he retired (the record has since been broken), and when he hit 40 in 1990 Sandberg became the first second baseman since Hornsby to lead the league.

For the hundreds of plays a second baseman is involved in, Sandberg rarely faltered in the field. In 1990, he committed just four errors in 157 games, and during a stretch from June 21, 1989, to May 17, 1990 (a span of 123 games), Sandberg did not commit a single fielding gaffe—a record for NL second basemen. His .989 lifetime fielding percentage is highest all-time among players who played at least 1,000 games at the position. He retired in 1994 at the age of 34 but soon realized he missed the diamond and unretired in 1996 to play two more solid seasons with the Cubs. He was inducted into the Hall of Fame in 2005.

Nobody has been able to fill Sandberg's shoes since he retired, at second base or anywhere else on the field.

*Ken Hubbs, 1962*

*Glenn Beckert, 1972*

**Left:** *Ryne Sandberg at bat, 1996*
**Below:** *Ryne Sandberg in the field, 1996*

*Joe Tinker, 1910*

# SHORTSTOPS

The first leg (poetically, anyway) of the legendary Tinker-Evers-Chance infield was also the one who had the longest tenure with the team. Joe Tinker's playing career in Chicago spanned 1,537 games, compared to 1,409 for Evers and 1,274 for Chance. Tinker arrived in 1902 and quickly earned the starting shortstop job, with mixed results. His 129 hits, 54 runs batted in, and 55 runs scored were second best on the team, but his 72 errors in 124 games at short showed that he had much to learn in the field. By 1908, Tinker was the top-fielding shortstop in the league, posting a .958 fielding average. His best offensive performance was in 1912, when he batted .282 and notched career highs in hits, runs, and RBI. He was traded to Cincinnati the following season and then jumped to the Federal League's Chicago Whales in 1914. When the Federal League folded after two seasons, Tinker returned to the Cubs as manager in 1916.

*Woody English, circa 1928*

Woody English was all about consistency on the Cubs infield in the late 1920s and early 1930s. He was a threat at the plate and in the field, twice batting above .300 and placing third in assists in 1929. He collected 214 hits, 100 walks, and 152 runs scored in 1930 while splitting time at short and third base. As a third baseman in 1933, English played in baseball's inaugural All-Star Game, but his production dropped in subsequent years, and he finished his career with the Dodgers.

English was spending most of his time at third base by 1932, the year that 24-year-old Billy Jurges took over the shortstop position. It wasn't quite a full-time gig for Jurges that season, however, since he missed nearly 40 games after being shot by a jealous ex-girlfriend in July. He recovered well enough in time to play in the World Series that year; he batted .364 in the series, more than a hundred points higher than his career average. Jurges played on two more pennant winners for Chicago, and his biggest contributions during his 1,072 games as a Cub were

*Billy Jurges, 1938*

with the glove. He was one of the top three fielding shortstops in the league every season from 1932 to 1938, before being traded to the New York Giants. He returned to Chicago in 1946 and 1947 as a part-time infielder and coach.

"It's a beautiful day for a ballgame. Let's play two!" Ernie Banks loved the game like few others, and on a summer day at Wrigley Field, why not play twice? Banks spent his entire career with the Cubs, from 1953 through 1970, starting at shortstop and later moving to first base—a superstar at each location. Banks was also the first black player to appear in a game for the Cubs. He finished behind Wally Moon in Rookie of the Year voting in 1954, but his .275 average and 19 homers were only a hint of things to come. In 1955, he pounded out 44 homers and drove in 117 runs, earning him his first of seven consecutive All-Star selections as a shortstop. (He also played in four "midsummer classics" as a first baseman.) He won back-to-back Most Valuable Player Awards in 1958 and 1959 playing for a team that languished in the bottom half of the standings. Banks whacked 47 home runs and 129 RBI in 1958, with a .313 average, and turned in an equally superb performance the next season (45, 143, .304). He had the best fielding percentage among NL shortstops in 1959, and he won a Gold Glove a year later.

Playing a position that traditionally favored speed and defense over power, Banks belted 277 of his 512 career homers as a shortstop—a record for the position that stood for more than two decades. Banks played more games in a Cubs uniform than anybody else in history. His 2,583 base hits and 1,636 RBI are second only to Cap Anson on the franchise list, and his 512 home runs trails only Sammy Sosa. Banks' uniform number 14 was the first one retired by the organization. He truly was "Mr. Cub."

Nobody spent more time at the shortstop position for the Cubs than Don Kessinger (1965–1975). A .252 career hitter who knocked a total of 14 homers in 16 seasons, Kessinger was primarily there for his superior glove work. Although he won only two Gold Glove Awards (1969 and 1970), he appeared in six All-Star Games. Kessinger rarely missed a game despite playing such a physically demanding position.

Ivan DeJesus was another workhorse at shortstop. After joining the Cubs in 1977, DeJesus led the club in games played in all but his first season (one game shy). He also was tops in stolen bases, hits, triples, and runs scored multiple times, and DeJesus complemented his offense with solid fielding. He appeared in every game of the strike-shortened 1981 season but

batted only .194. He was sent to the Phillies the next year—in the trade that brought Ryne Sandberg to Chicago.

Shawon Dunston was a high school phenom with a rifle arm when the Cubs made him the top pick in the 1982 amateur draft. A rookie in 1985, Dunston broke loose in 1986 with 145 hits, 68 RBI, and 17 homers. He led all NL shortstops in assists, putouts, and double plays. Dunston was known to ease into each season and improve as he went along, so fun-loving Cubs fans started the "Shawon-O-Meter," a sign that posted his batting average throughout the season. The streaky Dunston was a two-time All-Star, but injuries slowed him down by the mid-1990s.

*Ernie Banks, 1950s*

*Ernie Banks at the plate, 1960s*

*Don Kessinger, 1974*

*Shawon Dunston, 1997*

# DOUBLE-PLAY COMBOS

When the right combination of players comes together just right, those players, individually and as a group, can quickly rise to star status. One of the first winning infield combinations in baseball, and still one of the most celebrated, is the trio of Joe Tinker, Johnny Evers, and Frank Chance. When they arrived in Chicago, none of the three started at the position for which they later became famous. Manager Frank Selee was a shrewd judge of talent, however, and he shifted the players to where he thought they'd be most effective on the field. Chance moved to first base, Evers took second base, and Tinker moved to shortstop. The trio made their first appearance together on September 1, 1902, and on September 14, they turned their first double play, against the Reds in Cincinnati. Forty-four years later, Tinker, Evers, and Chance were inducted into the Hall of Fame together, in 1946.

Star players in their own right, the three gained near-mythological status in 1910 thanks to New York newspaper columnist Franklin Adams. After the Tinker-to-Evers-to-Chance squad snuffed a Giants rally at the Polo Grounds that July, Adams vented his frustrations in a poem entitled "Baseball's Sad Lexicon."

These are the saddest of possible words:
"Tinker to Evers to Chance."
Trio of bear cubs, and fleeter than birds,
Tinker and Evers and Chance.
Ruthlessly pricking our gonfalon bubble,
Making a Giant hit into a double—
Words that are heavy with nothing but trouble:
"Tinker to Evers to Chance."

Though not holding the same icon status, Chicago's infield of the mid-1930s had fan favorites around the horn: Phil Cavarretta at first, Billy Herman at second, Billy Jurges at short, and Stan Hack at third. The quartet was together for only two complete seasons (Cavarretta moved to the outfield for the next few years), but it was long enough to help win a pennant in 1935.

In the late 1960s, Chicago again had an all-star infield: Ron Santo at third base, Don Kessinger at shortstop, Glenn Beckert at second base, and the great Ernie Banks at first. The group was a feared defensive force, and all four played in the 1969 All-Star Game. They started as a unit in 1965 and combined to collect eight Gold Gloves (five for Santo) during their days together on the infield.

More recently, fans were treated to the awesome double-play threat of Dunston to Sandberg to Grace. The rifle arm of shortstop Shawon Dunston, the all-around greatness of second baseman Ryne Sandberg, and the consistent star-quality play of first baseman Mark Grace formed a powerhouse trio that menaced opponents during the late 1980s and early 1990s, and caught the spirit of Chicago's fans.

*Joe Tinker and Johnny Evers, 1911*

*Cubs infield, 1935*

*Ryne Sandberg and Shawon Dunston turn two against the New York Mets, 1989*

# Third Basemen

Ned Williamson played every infield position during his 13-year career; he also caught and pitched. But the position where he played the most, and had the most success, was at the hot corner. Williamson played third base for Chicago's first four pennant teams of the 1880s. He collected a total of 8 home runs through his first six years in the league and then exploded for 27 long balls in 1884—not the result of performance-enhancing drugs but rather a change in the ground rules at Chicago's Lakefront Park. (See "All-Time Home Run Hitters.") Williamson was also tops at his position in fielding percentage five times in seven seasons as the team's third baseman.

After Williamson shifted to shortstop in 1886, 11 different men held the third base job before Chicago would win its next pennant. Harry Steinfeldt came along just in time. Traded from Cincinnati before the 1906 season, he joined an infield that featured three future Hall of Famers and more than held his own. Steinfeldt led the league in hits, runs batted in, and fielding percentage; led the team in batting average (.327); and had a career-best 29 stolen bases. He never again batted above .300, but he continued as one of the better fielding third baggers throughout his time in Chicago.

The Cubs' first long-term, all-around star at the hot corner was Stan Hack, a solid defender and lifetime .301 hitter. "Smiling Stan" played his whole career in Chicago, and he came back to manage the club for three seasons in the 1950s. He twice led the NL in stolen bases and scored 100 runs or better in six consecutive seasons (1936–1941). He played on four World Series teams and turned in a .471 average in the 1938 Fall Classic. Hack briefly retired after the 1943 season, primarily because he couldn't get along with manager Jimmie Wilson, but changed his mind after Charlie Grimm became the manager and convinced Hack to come back. It paid off for Hack and Chicago. During the 1945 pennant season, Hack batted .323, scored 110 runs, and led NL third basemen in fielding. A five-time All-Star, he had speed on the base paths, a good eye at the plate, and a steady glove in the field, all of which helped to make him the premier third baseman of his day.

Stan Hack was a popular player with both fans and teammates, but it's hard to find a more revered third baseman in Chicago than Ron Santo. At the age of just 19, Santo tried out for the Cubs and, with a sterling recommendation from batting instructor Rogers Hornsby, was in the big leagues within a year. Santo played 95 games in 1960 and then missed only one game over the next five seasons; after appearing in 533 consecutive games, he missed the fourth game of the 1964 season and went on to start a new streak of 390 games. The nine-time All-Star belted at least 30 homers in every season from 1964 to 1967 while batting .302 over that span. He drove in more than 100 runs four times and averaged 92 RBI in 14 seasons with the Cubs. Santo's quick swing and patience at the plate helped him to lead the league in walks four times in five seasons (he finished second in 1965). In the field, Santo earned five consecutive Gold Gloves and was tops in assists and putouts seven times each. Battling diabetes since the age of 18, Santo had an unmatched determination to win, and he played every game like it was the championship. He left the club in 1973 and played his final season with the White Sox across town. He retired with 342 career home runs (337 of them with the Cubs), which ranks him fifth all-time among major league third basemen. Santo moved to the WGN radio broadcast booth in 1990, where he continues to captivate the Cubs faithful. His absence from the Hall of Fame is—in the eyes of many Chicagoans—one of the great travesties of Cooperstown.

The man charged with taking over for the beloved Santo at third base was certainly no slouch with the bat. Although he spent only three seasons with Chicago, Bill Madlock batted .336 during that time and won two batting titles, including a career-best .354 in 1975.

Another All-Star who took a brief turn at third for the Cubs was Ron "The Penguin" Cey, a 35-year-old veteran when the

*Ned Williamson, 1887 baseball card*

Dodgers traded him to Chicago in 1983. Cey drilled 24 home runs and drove in 90 runs in his first year as a Cub and proved it wasn't a fluke by amassing 25 homers and 97 RBI the following season. Cey also stepped it up with the glove, leading the league in fielding percentage.

Nobody was able to hold down the third-base job for more than one full season from 1995 to 2002, until Aramis Ramirez came over from the Pittsburgh Pirates midway through 2003. A native of the Dominican Republic, Ramirez signed with the Pirates in 1994 when he was just 16 years old and debuted in the majors at 19. The Cubs welcomed the young star while in the midst of a playoff hunt in 2003. Ramirez helped push Chicago to a division title, and he led the team in RBI in the postseason. Ramirez hit it big in September of 2004 when he belted three homers in a game against the Cincinnati Reds. Having accomplished the same feat against the Phillies in July, Ramirez became just the seventeenth player in major league history to have two three-homer games in the same season. He finished 2004 with impressive numbers (.318 average, 36 homers, 103 RBI, 99 runs). He was the starting third baseman in the 2005 All-Star Game and had another stellar campaign in 2006, belting 38 home runs and driving in 119 runs. Although he's not the strongest fielder at third, Ramirez has found a home in Chicago.

*Stan Hack, 1937*

*Harry Steinfeldt, 1908*

*Ron Santo in the field*

*Ron Santo at the plate*

*Bill Madlock, 1974*

*Aramis Ramirez, 2006*

# THE OUTFIELD

Every franchise has its list of all-star outfielders who played above the level of the competition year after year. It's much rarer to have a star at each outfield position at the same time, but the White Stockings of the 1880s were stacked left to right. When Chicago acquired 22-year-old Mike "King" Kelly from Cincinnati in 1880, he slotted into the right field spot alongside George Gore in center and Abner Dalrymple in left field—each one a budding star in his own right. Other than Kelly's brief turns at shortstop and catcher (as well as first base, second base, third base, and even pitcher), the Dalrymple-Gore-Kelly trio remained the outfield unit through the 1886 championship season.

Arguably the best all-around player of the nineteenth century, Kelly batted over .300 four times in his seven seasons with Chicago, including league-high marks of .354 in 1884 and .388 in 1886. Kelly was also a rocket around the bases. He led the league in runs scored in three straight seasons and was one of the top base stealers of his day. His mastery of the hook slide inspired the popular song "Slide, Kelly, Slide." Kelly lived large off the field, too, and the bottle caught up with him in 1886 when the tea-totaling Cap Anson sold him to Boston for the impressive (for the day) sum of $10,000.

George Gore and Abner Dalrymple both arrived in Chicago in 1879, and both were jettisoned, along with Kelly, by Anson after the 1886 season. Gore posted a league-high .360 batting average in 1880 and batted above .300 in six of his eight years with Chicago. Nicknamed "Piano Legs" for his powerful thighs, he stole seven bases in one game in 1881. Dalrymple, the least celebrated of Anson's outfielders, was a regular among the league leaders in base hits. In 1884, he took advantage of a temporary change in the ground rules at Lakefront Park and belted 22 homers; he retired in 1891 with 43 career home runs.

Frank Schulte, Jimmy Sheckard, and Jimmy Slagle constituted the outfield for the 1907 and 1908 World Champion Cubs. Although none achieved legendary status, Frank "Wildfire" Schulte, who had the longest tenure with the club (1904–1916),

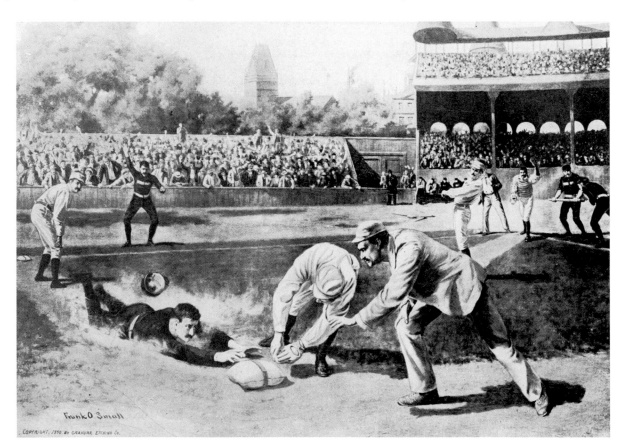

*King Kelly, sliding into second base, circa 1890*

was named the league's most valuable player in 1911 when he batted .300 and led the league in homers and RBI. He also became one of only five players in history to collect 20 doubles, 20 triples, and 20 homers in the same season.

Two-thirds of the Chicago Cubs outfield during the years 1928 to 1931 are currently enshrined in Cooperstown: Hack Wilson and Kiki Cuyler. The third, Riggs Stephenson, was a lifetime .336 hitter—best in franchise history. He batted over .360 two years in a row (1929 and 1930) and posted a .378 career average in World Series play with the 1929 and '32 Cubs. Center fielder Wilson rewrote the record books in 1930 when he smacked 56 homers and drove in 191 runs, the latter of which is still a major league record. He posted career bests with a .356 batting average and .723 slugging percentage while also receiving a league-high 105 bases on balls. Known as the year of the hitter, 1930 was a banner year for right fielder Cuyler as well. He had career marks in hits (228), runs (155), RBI (134), and doubles (50) while batting .355 and stealing a league-high 37 bases. The combined batting average of the starting outfield for the 1930 Cubs was .358.

More than one Chicago fan will declare that Billy Williams was the best left-handed hitter in team history—and his numbers

*Frank "Wildfire" Schulte, 1916*

*Riggs Stephenson, Kiki Cuyler, Rogers Hornsby, and Hack Wilson, 1930*

*Billy Williams, 1971*

*Andre Dawson, late 1980s*

are outstanding, indeed. Playing in the shadow of legendary figures like Ernie Banks, Ron Santo, and manager Leo Durocher in Chicago—not to mention Hank Aaron, Willie Mays, Roberto Clemente, and other Hall of Fame outfielders around the league—Williams was, in the words of Banks, one of the greatest hitters of all time and "one of the most underrated players ever." Williams' impact was immediate. In 1961, he turned in 25 home runs, 86 RBI, and a .278 average and walked home with the Rookie of the Year Award. The durable Williams played an NL-record 1,117 games in a row from 1962 to 1971. It's a toss-up as to which season was Williams' best. In 1970, he batted .322 and set career highs in hits (205), runs (137), homers (42), and RBI (129). In 1972, he established lifetime marks in batting (.333) and slugging (.606), both good enough for the league lead, while chipping in 37 homers and 122 RBI. He finished second to Cincinnati's Johnny Bench in the MVP voting both years and, remarkably, was not even named to the 1970 All-Star Team; he was a reserve in 1972. Williams played his final two seasons in Oakland but returned to Chicago as a coach after he retired in 1975.

The origin of Andre Dawson's nickname is debated, but a popular explanation is that it came from the motion of his swing

*Sammy Sosa, 2000*

*Alfonso Soriano and Jacque Jones, 2007*

and follow through. "The Hawk" perched his bat back above his shoulder, and it quickly took off, swooped down and back up again in an uppercut fashion. Already a superstar with the Montreal Expos, Dawson continued his superior play after signing with the Cubs as a free agent before the 1987 season. He took a pay cut to come to Chicago, and he paid it back with dividends. He led the league with 49 home runs and 137 RBI, was the starting center fielder in the All-Star Game, won his seventh (of eight) Gold Glove Award, and became the first player on a last-place team to win an MVP trophy. A five-time All-Star with the Cubbies, Dawson played in Chicago through the 1992 season and drove in more runs than any other teammate in all but one of those years (he finished two RBI short of Mark Grace in 1989).

Any list of all-time Cubs surely must include Sammy Sosa—speculation of steroid use and corked bats aside. In addition to his piles of home runs, Sosa had four seasons in which he batted above .300, and beginning in 1995, he ran off nine consecutive years with at least 100 runs batted in. Heralded as one of the game's great power hitters, Sosa's defense in the outfield was

as solid as Wrigley's outfield wall, and he was a stolen-base threat early in his career, leading the team in thefts every year from 1993 to 1995. (Known mostly for his long-ball prowess, his career is discussed further in the section "Home Run Kings.")

While today's outfield lacks anyone of the stature of a Sosa or a Williams, it does feature two former All-Stars in Alfonso Soriano and Cliff Floyd and a versatile speed-power threat in Jacque Jones. A six-time All-Star (through 2007), Soriano earned his $10-million salary in his first go-round with Chicago, leading the team in homers, runs, and slugging percentage and finishing second in stolen bases in 2007.

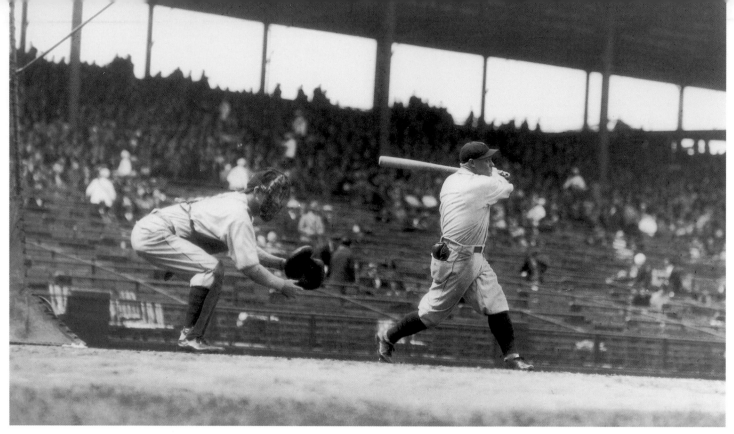

*Hack Wilson during batting practice, circa 1930*

# HOME RUN KINGS

Baseball before 1920 is generally regarded as the "dead-ball era"—but you wouldn't know it by looking at the 1884 Chicago White Stockings. Prior to that year, the National League's greatest single-season home run output was 10, by New York's Buck Ewing in 1883. In 1884, Chicago had four players with more than 20 homers, and King Kelly threw in another 13. The team hit a combined 142 homers; next best was Buffalo, with 39. The reason for the sudden

*Ned Williamson (far left) with the 1885 White Stockings*

power explosion was a change in the ground rules at Lakefront Park. Before and after 1884, balls hit over the park's absurdly close outfield walls (180 feet in left and 196 feet in right) were scored ground-rule doubles, but that year, they were considered home runs. Ned Williamson led the way with 27 dingers, which stood as the major league single-season record for 35 years. Over the other 12 seasons of his career, Williamson accumulated a total of 37 home runs.

Williamson held the franchise season record for more than 40 years, until venerable slugger Hack Wilson came along. Wilson was with the club for just six seasons, and he led the team in home runs in all but the final one. He broke Williamson's mark by hitting 30 in 1927, and he increased his output in each of the next three seasons: 31 in 1928, 39 in 1929, and 56 in 1930, the latter an NL record that stood for 68 years. A hard-playing, hard-partying man, Wilson could swat one out of the park with a flick of his wrist. He cranked 190 homers in just 850 games with Chicago.

Catcher Gabby Hartnett collected more than 30 home runs in a season only once (37 in 1930), but his consistency over 19 years with the club put him in the franchise's top spot for career home runs by the time he left Chicago in 1940. (He now ranks sixth.)

Bill Nicholson nearly left his mark, literally, on Wrigley Field when he narrowly missed the center field scoreboard with a towering home run in 1948. In fact, "Swish" Nicholson hit 205 homers for Chicago and led all teammates in his first eight full seasons there; he led all National Leaguers in 1943 and 1944.

Hank Sauer joined the Cubs a year after Nicholson left, and he was the team's main power source from 1949 to 1954, belting 198 homers in just over six seasons. Sauer averaged one home run for every 16 at bats as a Cub, second only to Sammy Sosa in home run proficiency on the all-time roster. The 1952 National League Most Valuable Player, Sauer hit 41 homers in 1954, as close as anyone got to Hack Wilson's number—until the arrival of "Mr. Cub."

As a 23-year-old rookie in 1954, Ernie Banks hit 19 home runs, tied for third-best on the team. The number leaped to 44 in 1955, and he had another 40-plus-homer season in 1957. And another in 1958. And another in 1959. And another in 1960. From 1955 through 1960—an era that starred the likes of Hank Aaron, Willie Mays, Frank Robinson, Mickey Mantle, Eddie Mathews, and Ted Williams—no major leaguer hit more home runs than Ernie Banks. On May 12, 1970, at Wrigley Field, Banks hit his 500th career home run, becoming the ninth player in history to join that elite group. He retired in 1971 with 512 lifetime homers, all with the Cubs.

*Bill "Swish" Nicholson*

*Sluggers Hank Sauer (left) and Ernie Banks (center) with Monte Irvin, 1956*

Various sluggers enjoyed the friendly confines of Wrigley Field during the 1970s and 1980s. In 1979, Dave "Kong" Kingman knocked 48 home runs, surpassing Banks' personal single-season peak of 47. (Kingman also flirted with another, less impressive team record by striking out 131 times.) Andre Dawson's 49 homers in 1987 inched closer to Hack Wilson's team mark, but over the next 20 years, no Cub hit more than 40 in a season.

Then, along came Sosa. Sammy Sosa stormed into Chicago in 1992 and spent the next 13 years beating up on opposing pitchers and piling up 545 home runs in a Cubs uniform. In his first full season in Chicago, 1993, Sosa burst out with a team-high 33 homers, the first of 13 consecutive years finishing among the NL's top ten. After averaging one home run in every 16 at bats from 1993 to 1997, Sosa belted out a phenomenal 66 homers in 643 at bats in 1998—a rate of one every 9.7 at bats. The long balls were accompanied by 158 RBI, 134 runs, and a .308 average in 1998. He hit a record 20 home runs in June alone. He won the 1998 MVP Award, beating out super-slugger Mark McGwire, and helped the Cubs reach the playoffs. In 1999, Sosa became the first player ever to hit more than 60 home runs twice in a career, and he did it again in 2001, when he had 64 homers, 160 RBI, 146

runs scored, a .328 average, and a franchise-record .737 slugging percentage. From 1998 to 2001, Sosa uncorked an *average* of 61 homers per season, and just shy of 150 RBI. He was traded to Baltimore in 2005 having hit more home runs than anyone in franchise history. Sosa and Banks are the only Cubs in baseball's 500-homer club.

In 2004, Sosa was one of four Cubs to hit at least 30 homers, along with Moises Alou, Aramis Ramirez, and Derrek Lee. Sosa and Alou were gone by 2005, but Ramirez and Lee kept the power flowing with a combined 77 homers between them.

*Dave Kingman, 1979*

*Sammy Sosa, 1998*

*Sammy Sosa and Ernie Banks, 2003 home opener*

*Aramis Ramirez and Derrek Lee, 2005*

# STARTING PITCHING

At the center of the baseball diamond, indeed the heart of the entire ballfield, the pitcher stands tall on the hill. With the spotlight on the mound, hurlers are bestowed with acclaim in victory and derision in defeat.

The pitcher's role in the game has changed significantly through the eras. In the sport's nascent years, most teams had a single starting pitcher in the same way that they had one starting first baseman or centerfielder. The starting pitcher was expected to pitch all nine innings of a game, and nearly every game over the course of the season. In 1876, Al Spalding started 60 of the White Stockings' 66 contests, logging in 528 of the total 592 innings played. By the next decade, starting pitching duties began to be shared, typically among two or three regulars.

The workhorses for Chicago in the early 1880s were Larry Corcoran and Fred Goldsmith. Corcoran boasted a blistering

*Wild Bill Hutchison, 1889*

*Larry Corcoran, 1880s*

fastball, and Goldsmith was one of the first to prefect the "curver." In order to preserve the arms of his star tandem, manager Cap Anson staggered their playing time—thus establishing baseball's first pitching rotation. The strategy paid off, as Goldsmith posted a phenomenal 21-3 record and 1.74 ERA in 1880, while the 20-year-old Corcoran earned 43 of the team's 67 victories and led the league in strikeouts. Corcoran is credited with being the first pitcher to develop signals with his catcher, and he is the only

*Mordecai Brown, 1909*

*Orval Overall, 1910*

Chicago hurler to throw three no-hitters in a career. Corcoran and Goldsmith accounted for 98 percent of the team's total innings pitched from 1880 to 1883.

For the first time in 1889, four different pitchers started at least 25 games and threw at least 200 innings for Chicago, led by Bill Hutchison. Hutchison's ace mantle was picked up by Clark Griffith—a six-time 20-game winner from 1894 to 1900—and by Jack Taylor, a four-time 20-game winner who completed 165 of the 167 games he started between 1898 and 1903.

Taylor was traded to Cincinnati after the 1903 season, and the Cubs got Mordecai Brown in return. Brown's arrival set the stage for a stellar staff that would help Chicago win four pennants by 1910. The addition of Ed Reulbach in 1905, Jack Pfiester before the 1906 season, and Orval Overall midway through 1906 gave the Cubs four starters who posted earned run averages below 2.00 in two consecutive seasons; Carl Lundgren made it five in 1907 with his 1.17 ERA. Overall won 23 games in 1907 and was the team's top strikeout pitcher in 1907, 1908, and 1909. Reulbach averaged about 19 wins a season from 1905 to 1909, and his .677 winning

percentage with the franchise trails only John Clarkson and Brown. As a group, the Cubs staff consistently compiled miniscule ERAs, including 1.75 marks in 1906 and 1910 and a 1.73 team ERA in 1907, a post-1900 record. Chicago held opponents to the lowest batting average every year from 1905 to 1911. In a change from previous decades, only twice did a pitcher log more than 300 innings in a season (Brown in 1908 and 1909), and manager Frank Chance was a pioneer in the use of the relief pitcher. Although the save was not an official statistic at the time, Brown led the league in that category four years in a row (1908–1911).

Chicago again led the league in pitching in its 1918 pennant season. Hippo Vaughn was the NL's ERA leader, and teammate Lefty Tyler was second, while Claude Hendrix's 20 wins were second to Vaughn's league-high 22. Hall of Famer Pete Alexander joined Vaughn in 1919 and helped guide the Cubs to another league-low ERA, but Chicago would then cease to be a dominating pitching force for over a decade.

The 1930s was the decade of the hitter, but the Cubs were able to balance the offensive explosion with solid pitching. The

As the Cubs settled into the long funk of second-division finishes, the pitching staff regularly allowed lots of hits and runs. The team's gradual climb back into the upper reaches of the standings toward the end of the 1960s—the so-called decade of the pitcher—was mostly thanks to offense. The bright spot on the mound was Ferguson Jenkins. The righty was called on for heavy duty, and he finished among the league's top five in innings pitched in every full season he spent in Chicago. Few other Cubs hurlers showed up on any leaderboards during this period. Even in the peak year of 1969, the Cubs had only the fifth-best team ERA in the 12-team National League.

During the 1980s, Chicago pitchers gave up more hits and more runs than any other team in the National League East, despite the two division crowns. They weren't much better in the 1990s. Kerry Wood brought some firepower in 1998 and in the first few years of the new century, and the emergence of Mark Prior, Matt Clement, and Carlos Zambrano, and the return of Greg Maddux, brought depth to the rotation. Injuries and failed expectations, however, left the team short. In 2007, Zambrano teamed up with lefties Ted Lilly and Rich Hill and righty Jason Marquis to anchor a premier staff in Chicago once again. The Cubs finished the season with the most strikeouts and the fewest hits allowed in the majors.

*Pitchers Joe Bush, Lon Warneke, Pat Malone, and Charley Root, 1932*

squad led the majors in ERA in all three pennant seasons and was well below the league average in hits allowed. The 1932 staff had four different pitchers who won 15 or more games, led by 22-game-winner Lon Warneke. In 1935, Warneke and Bill Lee became the team's first 20-win tandem since 1918, and in 1938 Lee paired with Charley Root to boast the league's two stingiest ERAs. The 1945 team showed its depth by taking the top three spots on the ERA list, led by Hank Borowy's 2.13.

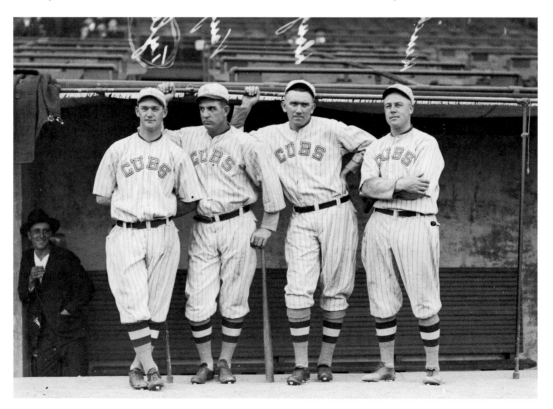

*Pitchers Lefty Tyler, Hippo Vaughn, Phil Douglas, and Claude Hendrix, 1918*

*Carlos Zambrano, 2007*

# RIGHT-HANDED ACES

The Cubs have a generous list of powerhouse right-handed pitchers, dating back to the nineteenth century. Following the Larry Corcoran–Fred Goldsmith duo of the early 1880s, John Clarkson unleashed an extraordinary performance in 1885. He won 53 games, threw 10 shutouts, struck out 308 batters, and pitched 623 innings—all league bests. The future Hall of Famer pitched more innings than anyone else in the league from 1885 to 1887 and completed 186 games in three and a half seasons in Chicago. Clarkson's .706 winning percentage is a franchise high.

Bill Hutchison pitched for Chicago from 1889 to 1895, and his 181 wins are third most on the franchise list; his 158 losses are first. He led the league in victories and complete games in three straight seasons (1890–1892) and is one of only five men in baseball history to win at least 40 games in two consecutive seasons. In just seven years with Chicago, "Wild Bill" pitched more innings than anyone else in franchise history except Charley Root, who spent sixteen years as a Cub.

*John Clarkson, 1887*

Leading off as one of the best pitchers in the twentieth century was Mordecai Brown, a sturdy Indiana farm kid who, despite a mangled right hand from a childhood accident involving a corn grinder, was a powerhouse pitcher for the better part of a decade. Brown amassed an impressive 1.80 earned run average in more than 2,300 innings with Chicago and tallied six consecutive 20-win seasons (1906–1911). He also led the league in saves from 1908 to 1911, and in 1909, he accomplished the rare feat of leading in wins, saves, and complete games in the same season. Brown holds the franchise mark for shutouts (48) and is second in wins (188). It is his ERA numbers, however, that are most startling. From 1906 to 1909, Brown posted earned run averages under 1.50 in four consecutive seasons, the only pitcher in major league history to accomplish such a feat. Almost as remarkably, his 1.04 mark in 1906 is the only time he led his league. Brown also pitched 20 combined innings in the 1907 and 1908 World Series and didn't allow a run.

Coming off three consecutive 30-win seasons in Philadelphia, Grover Cleveland "Pete" Alexander was acquired by Chicago before the 1918 season. He was drafted into the army early in the season but returned in 1919 and was the team's top pitcher for the next seven years. He led the league with a 1.72 ERA in 1919 and really hit his stride in 1920. He captured the pitching triple crown by leading in wins (27), ERA (1.91), and strikeouts (173). The hard-drinking, 39-year-old Alexander was released by Chicago in June 1926.

After Alexander, Guy Bush and Charley Root were Chicago's top hurlers for the next decade. Bush won 144 games from 1926 to 1934, while Root earned 15 or more victories eight times. Root's 201 career wins are the most by a Cubs pitcher—although he is perhaps best known for giving up the fabled "called shot" to Babe Ruth in the 1932 World Series.

The ace on Chicago's pennant teams of 1932 and 1935 was Lon Warneke, the "Arkansas Hummingbird." He paced the staff, and the league, with a 22-6 record and a 2.37 ERA in 1932, finishing second in the MVP voting that year. After winning 22 games again in 1934, Warneke mounted a third 20-win season in 1935.

In 1964, Larry Jackson (24-11) turned in the winningest season by a Cubs pitcher since Root won 26 in 1927. Less than two

*Mordecai "Three Finger" Brown's right hand, 1905*

*Charley Root, 1932*

*Lon Warneke at spring training, 1936*

years later, Jackson was traded to Philadelphia. In exchange, Chicago received its ace of the next seven years. A four-sport star at his Ontario high school, the six-foot-five-inch Ferguson Jenkins was at his peak in 1971. He went 24-13 with a 2.77 ERA and became the franchise's first Cy Young Award winner. With his ability to change speeds and his great control, he became the first major leaguer to strike out more than 250 batters while walking fewer than 40 in a season. Jenkins won 20 or more games in his first six seasons with the Cubs, but when the streak ended in 1973, he was traded to Texas. Fergie returned to Chicago to close out his career in 1982 and 1983. He retired as the franchise's all-time strikeout king. Jenkins was also the first Canadian-born inductee in baseball's Hall of Fame.

Rick "Big Daddy" Reuschel rolled in as the new ace for Chicago in the mid-1970s. The six-foot-three-inch, 235-pound Reuschel tallied nine consecutive years with double-digit victories—all at a time when the team didn't win many games. Rick's older brother Paul also played with the Cubs for four years, and in 1975, they became the first brother team to combine for a major league shutout, blanking the Dodgers 7-0.

To bolster its first run for the playoffs in many years, the Cubs acquired Rick Sutcliffe from Cleveland in June 1984. He posted a 16-1 record for Chicago over the remainder of the season and won the Cy Young Award. He re-signed with the team as a free agent, and in 1987 he led the NL in wins. That same year, the 21-year-old Greg Maddux—wearing Jenkins' old 31 uniform number—joined the starting rotation and struggled to a record of 6-14. He bounced back in 1988 (18-8, 3.18) and soon established himself as one of baseball's all-time best. In 1992, "Mad Dog" won his first of four straight Cy Young Awards (the latter three with Atlanta) when he went 20-11 with 199 strikeouts and a 2.18 earned run average. A winner of 16 Gold Glove Awards and a decent hitting pitcher, Maddux demonstrated unmatched versatility and effectiveness. After 11 seasons in Atlanta, Maddux was back in Chicago from 2004 through July of 2006 and added 38 more wins to his Hall of Fame stat sheet.

Chicago's next brush with pitching immortality came in 1998, when the 20-year-old Kerry Wood burst on the scene. In just his fifth major league start, the Texas phenom turned in one of the most dominant pitching performances in history. Wood

*Fergie Jenkins, 1969*

pummeled the Houston Astros with 20 strikeouts and allowed one hit and no walks in a complete-game shutout at Wrigley Field on May 6. Despite missing the last month due to arm trouble, Wood brought home the National League Rookie of the Year trophy. He missed all of 1999 after offseason elbow surgery, but he eventually returned to form. From 2001 to 2003, Wood struck out more than 200 batters each season and became the fastest pitcher to reach 1,000 career strikeouts in major league history. His career since then has been hampered by injuries.

At six feet, five inches tall and 255 pounds, Carlos Zambrano might look as comfortable in a Chicago Bears uniform as in a Cubs uniform. As it is, Zambrano is an imposing presence on the mound and has become Chicago's most consistent winner. He debuted in 2001 at the age of 20 and became a full-time member of the starting rotation in 2003. With an animated and emotional personality on the mound, "Big Z" has led the team in wins in every season from 2004 to 2007 and has struck out more opponents than any other Chicago hurler over the last five seasons. He is a threat at the plate, too, and in 2006, he became the first Cub pitcher to belt six homers in a season since Jenkins in 1971.

*Rick Reuschel, circa 1980*

*Greg Maddux, 1992*

*Kerry Wood, 2003*

# LEFT-HANDED ACES

In the early days of professional baseball, left-handed pitchers were a rare sight. The first documented lefty to pitch a game for Chicago was John Hibbard, who was on the hill for 17 innings in 1884 and yielded 18 hits and 10 runs. The team's first regular southpaw starter was George Van Haltren, who posted a 24-20 record for Chicago in 1887 and 1888. Lefty Gus Krock was the club leader in wins, earned run average, and strikeouts in 1888, but lefties remained an anomaly in the pitcher's box until the twentieth century.

Jack Pfiester was the first star southpaw on the Cubs staff. As a 28-year-old rookie in 1906, he lit it up with a 20-8 record and led the team in strikeouts. Pfiester posted a 15-5 lifetime record against the New York Giants, earning him the nickname "Jack the Giant Killer." He also pitched a complete-game win to give Chicago a 1-0 lead over Detroit in the 1907 World Series.

Widely regarded as the greatest left-handed pitcher in franchise history, James "Hippo" Vaughn loomed large on the mound with his six-foot-four-inch, 215-pound frame. Vaughn pitched five 20-win seasons for Chicago and ranks among the

*Hippo Vaughn, 1914*

franchise leaders in many categories. His pinnacle was 1918 when he won the pitching triple crown (leading in wins, ERA, and strikeouts). In a career loaded with highlights, one of Vaughn's most celebrated accomplishments was a double no-hitter he pitched with Cincinnati's Fred Toney on May 2, 1917. Both pitchers were flawless through nine innings, but the Reds finally managed to accumulate a couple of hits in the top of the tenth inning and won the game, 1-0.

The 1918 Cubs were in rare company when they acquired Lefty Tyler before the season, giving them two southpaws to anchor the staff. Tyler's 2.00 earned run average trailed only that of teammate Vaughn, marking the first time in history that two left-handed pitchers from the same team held the top two spots on the league leader board.

Two decades later, Larry French averaged 15 wins as the lone lefty in the rotation between 1935 and 1940. He was waived by the team while in the midst of a 5-14 season in 1941.

During the dark days of the early 1960s, Dick Ellsworth was a one-time 20-game winner for Chicago—and a two-time 20-game loser. Despite posting a respectable 3.70 ERA in seven seasons, his won-loss record with the Cubs was 84-110.

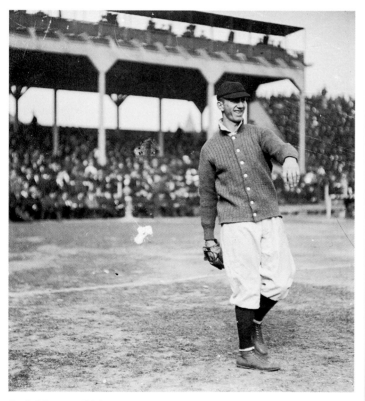

*Jack Pfiester, 1906*

In 1965, the Cubs drafted a young left-handed, Jewish pitcher. Although Ken Holtzman was not the second coming of Sandy Koufax, he did have a productive 15-year career, the first seven and last two of which were with Chicago. Holtzman won 17 games in 1969, and on August 19 of that year he pitched a no-hitter against the Braves, the first by a Cubs lefty. He repeated the feat 22 months later—on June 3, 1971, against Cincinnati—to become the first Cub since the 1880s to throw two no-hitters. The pitcher also scored Chicago's lone run in the game. Holtzman's best season-long outing in Chicago was 1970, when he went 17-11 and had a career-high 202 strikeouts.

In contrast to the lefties' thin ranks in the nineteenth century, the Cubs rotation in 2007 featured three regular southpaw starters—Ted Lilly, Rich Hill, and Sean Marshall—plus reliever Scott Eyre. In his first season with Chicago, Lilly posted a staff-best 3.83 ERA and won 15 games, while Hill was the strikeout king for the 2007 division champs.

*Larry French, 1935*

*Ted Lilly, 2007*

# RELIEVERS

Although starting pitchers continued to log heavy innings in the early twentieth century, the relief pitcher served an increasing role in game strategy, usually to bail out a struggling starter. Oftentimes, the ace relievers were simply the team's top starters, who did relief duty on their off days. Mordecai Brown started more games than any other Cubs pitcher during the years 1906 to 1910, and he also finished more games in relief than any other hurler. He led the league in saves for four straight seasons (1908–1911). In 1911, Brown started 27 games for Chicago (21 of which were complete-game outings) while finishing another 24 in relief. Brown's 13 saves that season stood as the single-season record until 1923, and his 49 lifetime saves stood as the major league high mark until 1925.

By the 1950s, relievers began assuming more specialized functions, but the league leaders typically amassed only about 10 to 20 saves in a season. Don Elston was Chicago's primary reliever between 1958 and 1964, appearing in more than 400 games

*Bruce Sutter, 1979*

*Mordecai Brown, 1911*

without starting a single one. He saved a total of 50 games from 1958 to 1962. Fifty saves in five years may be inconsequential by today's standards, but Elston was among the top five in the league in three of those seasons.

Lindy McDaniel became the first Chicago reliever to surpass 20 saves in a season, and his 22 saves in 1963 marked the first time a Cub led the league in saves since Guy Bush, who had eight in 1929. During his short tenure in Chicago, Ted Abernathy made a franchise-record 84 relief appearances in 1965 and set a new mark with 31 saves.

Various other relievers held the closing role for the Cubs in the late 1960s and early 1970s, until Bruce Sutter came along and broke open the record books. After notching 10 saves in his rookie season of 1976, he tied the franchise record with 31 in 1977. He busted loose two years later, collecting a league-high 37 saves and garnering the 1979 Cy Young Award. He won another saves title in 1980, but was traded to St. Louis in the offseason. Sutter spent only five years of his Hall of Fame career in Chicago, but he was an All-Star in four of them and employed his deadly split-fingered fastball to establish himself as one of the most dominant closers in baseball history. He saved 133 games for Chicago during a span in which the team won only 379 games.

*Guy Bush, circa 1929*

Bruce Sutter's role as ace closer in Chicago was soon filled by the intimidating and equally effective Lee Smith, a six-foot-six-inch force on the mound possessing a lethal fastball. Joining the team as a rookie in 1980, Smith led the NL with 29 saves in 1983. He then reeled off four consecutive years of 30 or more saves beginning in 1984, with a high of 36 in 1987, before being traded to Boston. Although his major league record for lifetime saves was broken by Trevor Hoffman in 2006, Smith still holds the Cubs franchise mark.

Over the last few decades, relievers' roles have gotten more and more specialized. Nowadays, bullpens are loaded with hurlers with one obligation—be it to come in and face a particular left- or right-handed batter, handle long-relief duties when a starter makes an early exit, take the middle innings, set up the closer, or come in to close the game and get the save, sometimes pitching only one inning or even to only one batter.

Before the 1993 season, the Cubs signed the hard-throwing lefty Randy Myers to be the team's closer. He appeared in 73 games that year and threw just 75.3 innings, an average of 1.03 innings per appearance. The arrangement seemed to work well,

*Rod Beck, 1998*

*Lee Smith, 1984*

as Myers promptly set a new National League record with 53 saves (since broken).

Only a handful of relievers have notched 50 or more saves in a single season, and the Cubs were fortunate to have another one come along in 1998. Rod Beck saved the day 51 times that year, including the clincher that secured Chicago a Wild Card spot in the postseason.

After spending his first six major league seasons as a starter, Ryan Dempster signed with the Cubs in 2004 and promptly was converted to a closer. He made the transition smoothly, amassing 85 saves in his first three full seasons in the role. Reliever Michael Wuertz has been effective in setting the table for closer Dempster. Since coming on board in 2004, Wuertz has a 3.59 ERA in more than 200 innings of work, all in relief. In 214 games as a reliever (through 2007), he has earned only one save. After two brief turns with the club in 2000 and 2001, Will Ohman rejoined Chicago's bullpen in 2005, where his primary obligation is to shut down opposing teams' left-handed hitters. He has appeared in 220 games and thrown 160 innings. He averages just three batters faced per appearance—illustrating the specialized roles that today's bullpen artists assume.

*Ryan Dempster, 2007*

# Bad Boys

Certain Chicago ballplayers from the team's early years were known to spend nearly as much time drinking, gambling, and brawling as they did playing ball. A fondness for the bottle afflicted more than a few prominent Cubs.

King Kelly is acknowledged as one of the top ballplayers of his day, and also one of the heavier drinkers. A dangerous force on the field throughout the 1880s, Kelly's wild living eventually got the best of him. He retired at the relatively young age of 35 due to alcohol-related health issues and died of pneumonia less than a year later. Several of Kelly's teammates, including Larry Corcoran, Ned Williamson, and catcher Silver Flint, were also renowned drinkers; all three died in their thirties.

*Pete Alexander, 1924*

Pitcher Pete Alexander bickered frequently with managers and teammates during his eight seasons in Chicago, and he reportedly showed up for games drunk or hung over on more than one occasion. Nevertheless, Alexander pitched effectively into his forties and is the fourth winningest pitcher in major league history.

Hack Wilson was a ferocious slugger who routinely blasted baseballs out of the park. He also didn't hesitate to land a blow with his fists to anyone unlucky enough to cross him. A five-foot-six-inch, 195-pound bull of a man, Wilson had a barrel chest and bulging arms that made him a force at the plate and in the barrooms. His affinity for a drink at a favorite watering hole was as renowned as his on-field prowess. Wilson's health suffered from his lifestyle, and he was out of the game by the time he was 34. He died in 1948 at age 48.

Gambling also tainted the careers of more than one Cubs player. Rogers Hornsby was one of the most successful hitters of all time, but he gambled, and lost, regularly at the horse track. He borrowed a lot of money from teammates, most of whom never saw their cash again. His gambling led to frequent clashes with the team brass and the league commissioner, Kenesaw Mountain Landis.

Although he was not known to be involved in any unsavory activity, Gabby Hartnett raised Commissioner Landis' ire when he signed an autograph for Sonny Capone, son of renowned Chicago gangster Al Capone, at a charity game in 1931. Landis wanted to eliminate even a hint of any connection between baseball and organized crime.

Claude Hendrix, who pitched for the Cubs from 1916 to 1920, was released from duty before the start of the 1921 season for allegedly betting against his own team. The previous August, Hendrix had been a last-minute scratch as starting pitcher against the Phillies when the team caught wind that gamblers were placing a lot of money on Philadelphia. The investigation into the Hendrix incident eventually focused on the 1919 World Series, but Hendrix never appeared in another major league game after 1920.

By comparison with baseball's rough-and-tumble early years, modern-day Cubbies have mostly steered clear of the tabloid scandal sheets. Even under increased media scrutiny,

*Hack Wilson's Home Run Club, a popular hangout for the swigging slugger*

*Claude Hendrix, 1918*

*Gabby Hartnett with Sonny and Al Capone, 1931*

strict league and club guidelines have helped to ensure that today's players toe the line. Every once in a while, however, emotions will get the better of a player, such as when the normally cool-tempered Derrek Lee lost his head against San Diego on June 16, 2007. After being hit by a pitch, Lee walked out to the mound to have some choice words with Padres hurler Chris Young. Words led to punches, and a bench-clearing brawl broke out. Lee and Young were both suspended for five games.

Intra-squad scuffles are usually best kept behind closed doors in the privacy of the clubhouse or team bus. Pitcher Carlos Zambrano and catcher Michael Barrett, however, aired their differences in full view of cameras and spectators in the Wrigley Field dugout during a game in 2007. The two had to be separated by coaches and teammates, and after they were shuffled off to the clubhouse, the shoving and slapping continued. Zambrano had apparently been frustrated with Barrett's fielding blunders and pitch selection during Chicago's 8-5 loss to Atlanta.

Things can get particularly ugly when the violence spills into the stands. Several Los Angeles Dodgers got into it with fans at Wrigley during a game on May 16, 2000, after unruly Cubs supporters tossed beer and other debris at visiting players sitting in the bullpen.

*Carlos Zambrano and Michael Barrett, in more peaceful times, 2007*

*Derrek Lee and San Diego's Chris Young, 2007*

Eighty years earlier, in the same ballpark and with the same teams on the field, Chicago's own Lefty Tyler had had enough of the taunts being hurled at them by a Dodgers fan in the crowd. Between games of the doubleheader, Tyler went and challenged the fan to "step outside the park" and threatened to rearrange his face. Tyler eventually cooled down, and the fan was promptly moved to another section of the stadium.

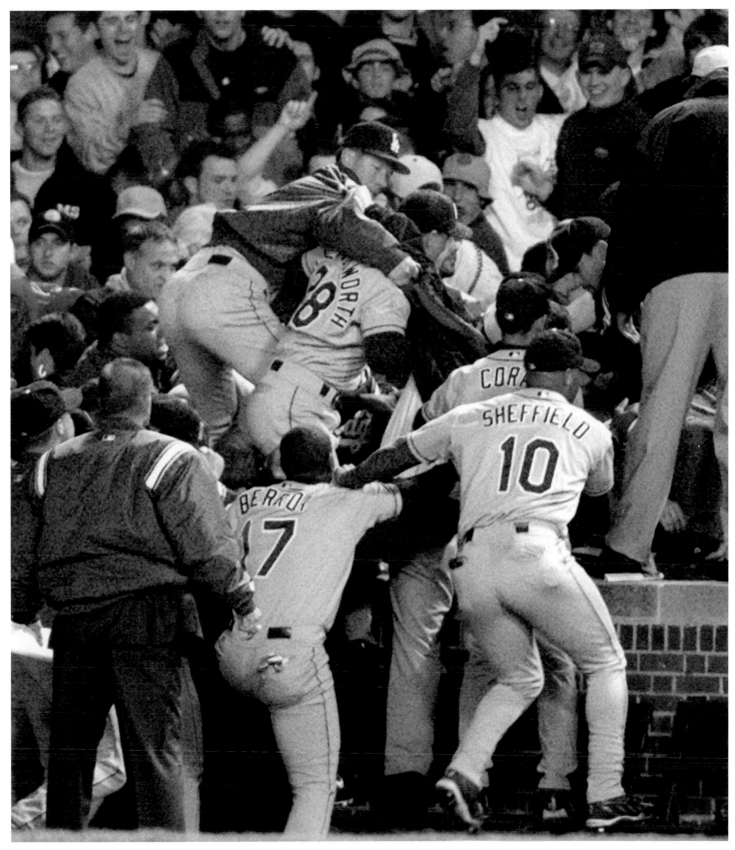

*Los Angeles Dodgers scuffling with fans at Wrigley Field, 2000*

# WINDY CITY RIVALRY

The Windy City's National League and American League franchises have been battling for bragging rights and fan loyalty ever since the Chicago White Sox came to town in 1900. When Charles Comiskey wanted to relocate his franchise from St. Paul to Chicago, the Cubs tried to block the move. They ultimately agreed, only on the condition that the new club make its home south of 35th Street. Comiskey's team adopted the old White Stockings name, which added more fuel to the rivalry fire. For more than a century, fans of the South Side Sox have rooted passionately against their North Side rivals, and the feeling is returned with equal gusto from the Cubs faithful. A common mantra is that the only thing the Cubs and White Sox have in common is the Red Line, the mass-transit route that passes both ballparks.

The Cubs and Sox first initiated a "City Series" in 1903, and until the institution of official interleague play in 1997, the two Chicago clubs met nearly every year at least once in exhibition play. The so-called Crosstown Classics were popular with the fans, even though the games did not count in the standings.

Both Chicago franchises had legendarily long stretches without a World Series appearance, but the two did meet head-to-head in the Fall Classic, once. The 1906 series attracted big crowds. Indeed, much of the city seemed to put business on hold that October as the Cubs and Sox battled it out. The series

*Program for City Series, Comiskey Park, July 11, 1949*

*Chicago City Series, West Side Grounds, October 10, 1910*

alternated ballparks for each game, with no days off between. The White Sox ultimately prevailed over the heavily favored Cubs in six games.

With the advent of interleague play, the Chicago clubs now meet annually in two three-game series, one at each park. The games sell out almost instantly, and these intra-city contests typically attract the largest crowds of the season. In the first interleague contest, on June 16, 1997, the teams went retro and donned 1906-style uniforms. The Cubs won the game, 8-3. The two have faced off in 60 official interleague contests (through 2007). The Cubs have won 30, and the White Sox have won 30.

There is certainly no love lost between the franchises, and the rivalry on the field is as hot as ever. During a Chicago vs. Chicago match on the South Side in May 2006, Cubs catcher Michael Barrett didn't take kindly to a hard slide by his White Sox counterpart, A. J. Pierzynski. Barrett responded with a punch to Pierzynski's jaw, and an all-out melee ensued. It took more than fifteen minutes for order to be restored. Four players were ejected, Barrett eventually earned a 10-game suspension, and adding insult to injury, the White Sox blasted the Cubs 7-0 in the game.

Despite the occasional ugliness, for the most part it is a good-natured rivalry between neighbors. Many contend that the White Sox have always been considered the city's "second" team. Cubs fans heartily agree, but Sox supporters will quickly point to their 2005 World Series victory as a sign that they are, in fact, Chicago's number one team. A White Sox fan at a 2006 interleague game made sure to remind Cubs supporters of their past history with a large sign proclaiming "1906."

*Ryne Sandberg and White Sox third baseman Ozzie Guillen, June 16, 1997*

*Fans at Cubs–White Sox game, U.S. Cellular Field, May 19, 2006*

*Michael Barrett and A. J. Pierzynski, May 20, 2006*

# UNIFORMS AND EQUIPMENT

According to uniform expert Marc Okkonen, author of *Baseball Uniforms of the 20th Century*, professional baseball teams have donned more than 4,000 different uniform styles since 1876. The Chicago Cubs have done their part, with dozens of variations from the club's inception to the present day.

Chicago ballplayers of the early years looked rather dashing on the field, wearing collared shirts with ties, long pants, and lace-up boots. By the time the National League was formed, knickers had supplanted full-length pants, and Chicago's players wore white socks below the knee. Identifying marks on home and road shirts were also introduced, with some uniforms simply plain white or gray and others bearing the word "Chicago" across the chest.

*Chicago White Stockings, 1888*

Lace-front shirts gave way to buttons by the late 1890s, and in 1937, the Cubs became the first team to wear a zippered shirt. The zipper remained until the mid-1950s. The full collar was replaced by a cadet-style stand-up collar in 1909, then shirts went collarless in the 1920s.

Solid white and gray uniforms were the norm for most of the first half of the twentieth century, although the Cubs did mix in some deviations. In the early 1910s, the team wore dark blue uniforms when playing on the road, and they dabbled with pinstripes at various points—including red stripes in 1918. A design innovation that was first unveiled in Chicago in 1940 was the sleeveless vest over a solid-colored, long-sleeved undershirt, as modeled by outfielder Lou Novikoff on the facing page. While the Cubs stuck with the style for only three seasons, other teams retained the vest look well into the 1960s. (It has been reintroduced by several clubs in the last decade or so.) Blue pinstripes returned to Chicago's home uniforms in 1957 and have remained part of the wardrobe ever since. When other teams experimented with vibrant colors in the 1970s, the Cubs went with a pale blue hue for the road attire, in both solid and pinstriped varieties. In 1982, the team switched to dark blue jerseys with white pants on the road. The V-neck pullover jersey also came into vogue from 1972 to 1989, but by 1990, the uniform returned to a more classic look: white and gray background colors, button-down shirts, and belted pants. The team also continues to don the occasional

*Fred Pfeffer, 1887*

alternate outfits, such as the solid blue shirt sported by shortstop Alex Gonzalez in 2003 (see page 99).

The logo and lettering on the uniform jerseys have also seen numerous variations. A large, old-English-style "C" appeared on the left breast pocket during the 1903 season; a more rounded letter was used on home jerseys in 1906 and 1907, while the word "Chicago" ran across the chest of road uniforms. The bear figure was introduced inside the "C" in 1908, and the logo has taken several forms over the past century. In its first incarnation, the bear stood on its hind legs holding a bat. The bear moved to the shirt sleeve for 1914, and then returned to the left breast in 1916, this time on all fours. The upright-standing bear reclaimed its

**Above:** *Tiny Osborne, circa 1922*
**Right:** *Lou Novikoff, 1940*

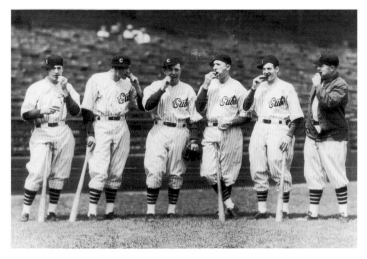

*Cubs players, circa 1931*

*Dizzy Dean and Gabby Hartnett, 1938*

spot inside the "C" on home uniforms in the 1920s. (In 1934, it took a pitching pose on one version of the home attire.) After being omitted from the everyday uniforms for most of the 1940s and 1950s, the bear showed up on the sleeve again in 1962, where it has remained ever since. Initially a cartoony head shot, as seen here on Ron Santo's 1967 pose, the bear went to all fours in the mid-1990s. It also appears on the breast of the alternate blue jerseys.

The team's nickname made its debut on the uniforms in 1909, when the letters "UBS" were printed inside a large "C" on road uniforms (where the bear resided on the home version). In 1909, the word "Chicago" also ran down the button panel on the road jersey, as modeled by Johnny Evers below. A more straightforward spelling of "Cubs" was used intermittently from 1913 to 1925, in different typefaces. In the early 1930s, the club experimented with elaborate script for the word "Cubs" on home uniforms, while the road shirts featured a script "Chicago" across the chest and a script "Cubs" on the sleeve. By the end of the 1930s, a rounded red "C" surrounding the letters "UBS" on home uniforms and the word "Chicago" above a curved line for the road outfit were the standard looks for years to come. The encircled Cubs logo was used both home and away from 1982 to 1989. Today, the big red C emblem inside the blue circle is a recognizable icon to Cubs fans everywhere.

**Left:** *Ron Santo, 1967*

*Johnny Evers in road uniform, 1909*

*Jimmy Archer in road uniform, 1910*

*Heinie Zimmerman in road uniform, 1912*

Dick Tidrow, circa 1981

Antonio Alfonseca in home uniform, 2003

Sammy Sosa in road uniform, 2000

Alex Gonzalez in alternate uniform, 2003

Much of baseball's allure can be credited to its simplicity. Minimal gear is required, and back in the day, professional players carried little more than did the kids at the local sandlot. Past and present players owe thanks to Chicago's own Albert Spalding for revolutionizing the game with the introduction of the glove. Prior to the 1870s, cannon-blast line drives were fielded barehanded. Early in the 1877 season, having shifted from pitcher to first base, Spalding began wearing a black, fingerless, leather glove with a padded palm in the field. Players who previously tried to protect their hands had endured heckling from fans and even their own teammates. But Spalding was revered by fans and respected throughout the league, and soon other players were asking where they could get a glove like his. Conveniently enough, Spalding's sporting goods emporium in Chicago sold the gloves (for around $3.00), and business boomed.

Glove design improved greatly in ensuing decades, evolving from the thin horsehide models of Spalding's day to a full-fingered, padded mitt in the early 1900s. The webbing between the thumb and forefinger came along by the 1920s. With minor modifications, the same basic design is seen in today's fielding gloves.

It is the catcher who has perhaps benefited the most from advances in protection. Like their teammates on the field, catchers strived to maintain a tough-guy image and typically took the field with no protection. By the late 1800s, when overhand pitching was legalized, the potential for broken fingers or a fastball to the noggin had greatly increased. In 1887, catcher Silver Flint strikes a pose that illustrates the rather rudimentary protection afforded by the early versions of a glove and mask. Catcher's mitts rapidly evolved from thin gloves to bulbous mittens of padding and horsehide, and eventually deeper pockets. At spring training in the late 1930s, Hall of Fame catcher-manager Gabby Hartnett coached a couple of young teammates, who wear the bigger gloves, along with lightweight chest and shin protectors common to the day.

By comparison to their counterparts of previous decades, today's catchers are loaded head to toe with high-tech gear. Carbon helmets, indestructible plastic shin guards, and streamlined chest protectors provide both the defense and mobility required by the modern game.

*Silver Flint, 1887*

*Gabby Hartnett
with catchers-in-
training, 1939*

*Jody Davis, 1980s*

*Michael Barrett, 2007*

# EARLY BALLPARKS

Before there was Wrigley Field, five different ballparks hosted Chicago's National League franchise, dating back to 1876. The team's first home was the 23rd Street Grounds, which had also been the White Stockings' quarters in the final two seasons of the National Association. The tumbledown facility featured a small, 1,500-seat grandstand, a short outfield, and a rickety six-foot fence on the perimeter to prevent fans from watching games for free. The White Stockings posted a 42-18 home record in two seasons at 23rd Street Grounds.

The team upgraded to Lakefront Park before the 1878 campaign. Situated in downtown Chicago near the shores of Lake Michigan, the ballpark was located at the site of the earlier Union Base-Ball Grounds, where the National Association's White Stockings played in 1871 until the Great Chicago Fire laid waste to the ballpark. The lavish Lakefront Park is considered the first major league stadium to feature luxury boxes. Several private boxes were perched atop the grandstand; owner Al Spalding's personal suite boasted a telephone and a gong to summon waiters. Lakefront Park also had a bicycle track encircling the field. The ballpark could accommodate about 3,000 fans, but a day at Lakefront was not always a luxurious experience. Debris from the Great Fire had been dumped on the site, and winds from Lake Michigan would often swirl dust from the ashes, and smoke and cinders from adjacent railroad yards, into the stands. Players had to contend with glass, rocks, and other detritus embedded in the field. Still, the team seemed unfazed by the conditions, unleashing three straight pennants from 1880 to 1882. The outfield dimensions were very short at the park, and until 1884, balls hit over the fence were ruled ground-rule doubles.

*Lakefront Park, circa 1884*

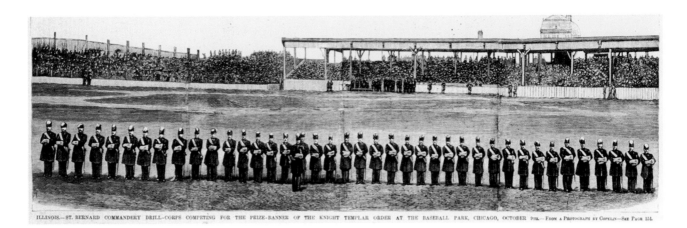

ILLINOIS.—ST. BERNARD COMMANDERY DRILL-CORPS COMPETING FOR THE PRIZE-BANNER OF THE KNIGHT TEMPLAR ORDER AT THE BASEBALL PARK, CHICAGO, OCTOBER 9TH.—FROM A PHOTOGRAPH BY COPELIN—SEE PAGE 151.

*Lakefront Park, during a gathering of the Knights Templar, 1882*

(Chicago regularly led the league in doubles.) In what proved to be a one-year experiment, over-the-fence hits were ruled home runs during 1884, leading to record-breaking numbers of home runs hit at Lakefront Park that season. It would be the White Stockings' final season at the ballpark.

The club played the first 24 games of the 1885 season on the road while a new ballpark was being built west of downtown. Chicago hosted its first game at West Side Park on June 6, 1885, and proceeded to rattle off a 14-game winning streak. They finished the season with a record of 44-14 at home en route to another pennant. Though not as intimate as Lakefront, West Side Park also had short distances to the outfield, and the team continued to lead the league in home runs every season from 1885 to 1891. The new park was a hit with fans, too. It featured seating for about 10,000, painted woodwork, a brick wall on the perimeter, and lavish private roof boxes for the well-to-do. Fans traveling to games by horse-drawn carriage could roll through a covered entrance and park in deep center field.

In 1891, the Chicago Colts (as they were then known) split their games between West Side Park and a facility on Chicago's South Side, where the Chicago Pirates of the short-lived Players' League had played in 1890. The Colts played at West Side Park on Mondays, Wednesdays, and Fridays and moved to South Side Park for games held on Tuesdays, Thursdays, and Saturdays. South Side Park became the regular home in 1892, and in 1893, all Sunday contests were held at a newly constructed West Side

Baseball Game in West Side Ball Grounds, Chicago.

*Postcard view of West Side Grounds, 1908*

Grounds, which replaced the previous ballpark located a few blocks away.

The Colts moved to the West Side Grounds full time in 1894 and remained there through 1915. This new park was the best thing going for Chicago fans, who couldn't seem to get enough of their hometown heroes. The facility had a double-deck grandstand, among the first of its kind in the major leagues, and could hold about 16,000 spectators in the grandstand and open stands that extended down the foul lines. (The main grandstand was partially damaged by fire during a game in August of 1894 and later rebuilt.) Indeed, even the enlarged seating capacity could not satisfy all the team's supporters, and—foreshadowing a later tradition at Wrigley Field—several buildings across the street sported makeshift seating on the rooftops, from which fans could catch a free view of the action. By 1915, the team owners grew weary of all the free onlookers and enclosed the outfield with tall billboards.

The ballpark was regularly attracting full crowds by the early 1900s, and in 1905 the grandstand was expanded with the addition of rooftop boxes behind home plate. A columned clubhouse building stood in deepest center field. As the team entered its dynasty era, seating sections along the first- and third-base lines were covered, more private boxes were added to the infield grandstand, and an outfield bleacher section was constructed. Fans filled temporary seating in the outer reaches of the outfield for big games, of which the Cubs of 1906–1910 had many.

The Cubs played their final regular-season game at West Side Grounds on October 3, 1915, earning a 7-2 win over the Cardinals. After the team departed for Weeghman Park (Wrigley Field), the old facility was used by amateur teams until it was torn down in 1920. Today, the site is home to the University of Illinois Medical Center.

*View of West Side Grounds from grandstand, 1910*

*Cubs warming up before a game, West Side Grounds, 1908*

# WRIGLEY FIELD

Perhaps the seminary once located here provided the inspiration that has led to Wrigley Field's status as one of baseball's most hallowed ballparks. Charles Weeghman, owner of the Federal League Chicago Whales, was determined to provide his club and fans with a superlative facility to compete with the other major league clubs. He secured the seminary property in 1913 and immediately began construction of a "park to outshine any other." Weeghman Park opened in April 1914. Originally accommodating 14,000 fans, by 1915 the single-deck grandstand seated 16,000, with room for another 2,000 in the right-field bleachers. The Federal League folded after the 1915 season, but Weeghman took the

*Postcard view of Wrigley Field, early 1940s*

opportunity to purchase controlling interest in the Cubs. He wasted no time moving the team from the aging West Side Grounds to his new park. The Cubs played their first game there on April 20, 1916, and defeated the visiting Cincinnati Reds, 7-6.

When William Wrigley assumed ownership, he renamed the stadium Cubs Park in 1920 and quickly set out to make it bigger and better. The grandstand was expanded before the 1923 season, and a second deck was added in 1927 and 1928, increasing the capacity to more than 38,000. The park was rechristened Wrigley Field in 1926.

William's son and successor, Philip Knight Wrigley, was further committed to improving the ballpark. A major renovation in 1937 included the construction of new outfield bleachers and a new scoreboard. Perhaps most famously, P. K. Wrigley collaborated with Bill Veeck Jr. to decorate the outfield wall with ivy.

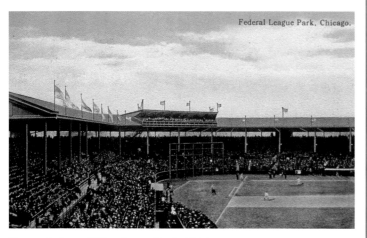

*Postcard view of Weeghman Park, 1914*

Other than some minor renovations, such as updated clubhouses for players and additional luxury boxes, Wrigley Field remained largely unchanged for the next half century. A revolutionary change came to Wrigley in the late 1980s—about 40 years after other teams took the leap. In 1938, Cincinnati's Crosley Field became the first major league park to install lights for night baseball. Others quickly followed suit, and the Cubs were preparing to do the same after the 1941 season. But with the attack on Pearl Harbor that December and the nation's march to war, Philip Wrigley donated the materials to the war effort. The lighting project was put on hold, indefinitely.

*Game one, 1938 World Series, Wrigley Field*

When the Tribune Company purchased the Cubs in 1981, the new owners began battling neighborhood groups and the city to install lights. When the league threatened that the Cubs would have to play any postseason games at other venues, lights were finally installed at Wrigley in 1988. The first night game was scheduled for August 8. Mother Nature was apparently not in favor of night baseball at Wrigley, however, and the game was called on account of rain in the fourth inning. The first official night game took place the following evening against the New York Mets.

A $13.5-million project to update the bleachers prior to the 2006 season is the most recent round of updates to the storied park. Despite various improvements and updates over the years, Wrigley Field remains a classic ballpark evoking an earlier era. It lacks certain amenities, such as dedicated parking, and some seats may be obstructed by the ancient pillars holding up the second deck. But Wrigley remains a landmark of the sport—and nothing beats hearing the crack of the bat on a warm summer afternoon at Wrigley Field.

*Wrigley Field, 2005*

**Above:** *Wrigley Field, 1930s*

**Right:** *Wrigley Field exterior, 1930s*

**Above:** *Wrigley Field, 2007*

**Left:** *Wrigley Field exterior, 2007*

# BLEACHER BUMS

Though the ballpark has been updated with ample luxury suites in recent decades, and the rich and famous can often be seen viewing the action from their private boxes, a no-frills bleacher seat remains a hot ticket at Wrigley Field. For many, the bleachers is the only true way to experience a Cubs game.

When the Cubs first moved to Weeghman Park in 1916, a wooden bleacher section extended across left field from the foul pole to the center-field scoreboard. During the ballpark revamp prior to the 1923 season, a new bleacher section was built in right field, and the left field section was updated. The reorientation of the field, however, meant that the left-field bleachers were just 325 feet from home plate, making an all-too-easy home run target, and by 1925, the section was reduced to a small "jury box" area in deepest left-center. For the 1929 World Series, William Wrigley had temporary bleacher sections built atop the outer walls of the ballpark, extending onto Waveland and Sheffield Avenues.

The bleachers were completely overhauled before the 1938 season. The new, durable concrete seating section did not extend all the way to the corners of the outfield, which created small "wells" between the bleachers and the foul pole. This anomaly made Wrigley the only ballpark where the distance from home plate is greater at the foul poles than it is inside the field of play. The lower bleacher section in straightaway center field was closed to spectators when it was discovered that the white-shirted fans created a difficult background for hitters. The area was eventually filled in with junipers and other evergreens.

Another major renovation of the bleachers in 2006 added some 1,800 seats in left and right field, including a 250-seat "Bleacher Box" section in right. The "Batter's Eye" luxury suite was built in the lower center field area, and the bleacher section was redubbed the "Bud Light Bleachers."

Back in the early 1960s, the bleachers were not always the scene of a lot of action at Wrigley, as is evident during a late-season contest between the seventh-place Cubs and the eighth-place Phillies in 1961. Other times, though, the bleachers is where you will find some of the team's rowdiest supporters, such as the group that showered the field with beer cups and other debris to protest an umpire's call during a 1999 game.

The mystique of Wrigley's bleachers inspired a stage play, called *Bleacher Bums*, that debuted in 1977 and later aired on public television. The play, which starred Joe Mantegna and Dennis Franz in its initial run, highlighted the passion, camaraderie, and beer drinking of a typical bleacher crowd.

*Right-field and temporary bleachers, Wrigley Field, 1929 World Series*

*Bleacher renovation, 2006*

**Above:** *Bleacher crowd, 1961*

**Right:** *Bleacher crowd, 1999*

*Bleachers, circa 2005*

# THE OUTFIELD WALL

For all of Wrigley Field's laurels, the ballpark's most cherished ornament is the outfield wall. From humble beginnings as the park's boundary, the brick fence's leafy visage now holds celebrity status throughout the sports world.

At West Side Grounds, the outer reaches of the playing field were surrounded by a simple wooden or chain-link fence. The dominant features of the outfield vista were the billboards where local advertisers hawked everything from cigarettes and booze to hats and underwear. For many years, the Chicago *Tribune* dominated the ballpark skyline with a large billboard in right field touting the paper's sportswriters. In the early 1910s, owner Charles Murphy increased the height of the outer walls around the rest of the outfield, which served the dual purpose of providing more space for advertisements while also blocking out the

wildcat bleachers across the street. By 1915, the entire outfield was enclosed by giant billboards, with the *Tribune* ad now looming in left field. Among the messages being communicated to the fans was a sign warning, "No Betting Allowed."

When the Cubs relocated to their new home in 1916, the outfielders needed to adjust in a hurry to the more substantial brick barrier around the Wrigley Field outfield. To soften the blow (ever so slightly), vegetation would later be the sole cushioning placed on the walls. In the late 1930s, owner P. K. Wrigley desired a park-like ambiance, and he charged the young Bill Veeck to make it so. Inspired by the ivy walls of Perry Stadium in Indianapolis and at the White Sox's spring training facility in Pasadena, Veeck began plans to decorate his home stadium with a similar look after the 1937 season. The deadline was moved up considerably, however, when Wrigley announced that he would

*West Side Grounds, showing outfield billboards, 1915*

*Groundskeepers planting ivy, September 1937*

have guests arriving to see the ivy before the season's last home series. Veeck scrambled and brought in several hundred fast-growing bittersweet plants to grow along with the ivy. The grounds crew worked feverishly to plant the bittersweet on wires strung along the wall. The next day, the ballpark had a new feel—the entire wall was draped in a leafy cloak. The ivy eventually filled in, and today it is the most famous foliage in Chicago. Hoping to add to the arboretum effect, Veeck also set up large planters with Chinese elm trees on the large stair-steps leading up to the new scoreboard, but the wind wreaked havoc on the trees, and that component of the Wrigley beautification project was abandoned.

The ivy provides only minimal padding for outfielders leaping for fly balls against the wall, and it brings an added obstacle when balls disappear into the green abyss. According to the Wrigley Field ground rules, if a ball is hit into the ivy and is lodged there, it is ruled a double as long as the outfielder indicates to the umpire that the ball has disappeared. If, however, the outfielder attempts to retrieve the ball from the ivy, then the ball is considered live.

Another distinct element of the Wrigley outfield wall is the bright yellow measurements indicating the outfield distances. Initially plywood markers attached to the wall, the dimensions have been painted directly on the brick since 1981. The screen on top of the wall was added in 1970 to minimize the instances of fan interference. A ball that gets lodged in the screen is ruled a double, but if it bounces off the screen and into the bleachers, it's a home run.

One thing you won't see adorning the walls of the Friendly Confines, however, is much billboard advertising. In today's era of heavy corporate sponsorship—where every piece of the game is seemingly for sale to the highest bidder, from the ballpark name to the seventh-inning stretch—Wrigley Field remains remarkably free of commercial advertising inside the bowl. The video scoreboard does feature corporate sponsors, but most of the large billboards are left to the buildings across the street. A sign advertising Baby Ruth candy bars towered above a building in center field for decades. Today, the roof of a Waveland Avenue building beyond left field is painted with the bright red-and-white Budweiser logo.

*Sammy Sosa, 2003*

*Houston outfielders Lance Berkman and Hunter Pence, 2007*

*Distance measurement painted on left-field wall*

# THE SCOREBOARD

High above the ivy is another Wrigley Field treasure. The manual scoreboard towering above the centerfield bleachers has been in use for more than 70 years, the oldest scoreboard in the majors. Game scores and pitcher numbers are still changed by hand, while other stats have gone electronic.

The ballpark's previous scoreboard in center was topped by two Wrigley gum "stick men"—a pitcher and a batter—and the board provided inning-by-inning scores for all the games around the league. Workers began dismantling the old scoreboard and bleacher section in late 1937 as part of a stadium renovation project.

*Wrigley Field with old scoreboard, Opening Day, April 1937*

*Whales player Max Flack in front of scoreboard at Weeghman Park, 1914*

While the inning-by-inning score and pitching changes are updated by hand, the new scoreboard employs magnetic covers to display batters' uniform numbers and updates on balls, strikes, and outs. This was an innovative design at the time, and one not previously used in the major leagues. A precursor to the digital age, each 18-inch-by-30-inch opening is made up of a collection of 4-inch holes covering a white background panel, and a hand-operated lever opens the appropriate "eyelets" to display the desired numbers. A 10-foot diameter clock was added to the top of the board in 1941, but otherwise, little has changed. Today, the batter's stats are displayed electronically at the base of the scoreboard, with the rest of the board still operated manually.

The 27-foot-high by 75-foot-wide scoreboard is an enticing target for batters, although no slugger has managed to knock one off the big green board, yet. There have been a few close calls, most notably Bill Nicholson in 1948 and Roberto Clemente in 1959. For now, a legend from another sport holds the honor of being the only person to hit the scoreboard with a ball—in this case, a golf ball. Golfer Sam Snead teed one up at home plate and nailed the board.

Another long-standing Wrigley tradition flies above the scoreboard. After each game, a Cubbies win is announced with a white flag bearing a blue "W"; a loss is noted with a blue flag and a white "L." (Previously, losses had been indicated with a white flag, but since a white flag is also a symbol of surrender, the colors were swapped.) Also above the scoreboard, banners for each National League team are arranged according to the teams' place in the standings. White flags at the left- and right-field foul poles bear the retired uniform numbers of Ernie Banks, Ron Santo, Billy Williams, and Ryne Sandberg, four all-time greats and Chicago heroes.

**Above:** *Completed scoreboard, October 1937*
**Left:** *Scoreboard under construction, July 1937*

*Scoreboard, circa 2005*

# THE PLAYING FIELD

The diamond shape of a baseball field has changed little since Alexander Cartwright of the New York Knickerbockers issued a set of rules in 1845 establishing distances of 42 paces between home plate and second base and between first base and third. The dimensions were formally changed to 90 feet between bases at the First Convention of Base Ball Clubs in 1857. Early ball fields, including West Side Grounds, commonly had a "keyhole" design that featured a dirt "running lane" for the catcher between home plate and the pitcher's spot.

Maintaining the condition of the turf and base paths can be an art form. Indeed, Bill Veeck once commented that a good grounds crew can win you 10 to 12 games a season. The length of the grass, the dampness of the dirt, and the firmness of the mound can all be adjusted, subtly, by the home-field crew to maximize the strengths and minimize the weaknesses of the home team. Bobby Dorr was the master groundskeeper at Wrigley Field during the 1920s and 1930s, a time before high-tech landscaping and irrigation tools. Dorr was so dedicated to his job, in fact, that he lived in a six-room apartment under the seats near the left-field corner gate.

At the center of the diamond, pitchers in nineteenth-century baseball threw from ground level with the batter. They also stood only 45 feet away, according to the rules of the 1857 Convention of Base Ball Clubs. The distance was increased in

*Jack Pfeister, 1906 World Series, West Side Grounds*

*West Side Grounds, 1907*

stages during the 1880s, until the current distance of 60 feet, 6 inches was introduced in 1893. In 1904, the pitcher's plate gave way to a raised pitcher's mound. An early incarnation of the mound is evident in the image of Jack Pfeister delivering a pitch during the 1906 World Series. The maximum mound height was originally set at 15 inches, and pitchers enjoyed this advantage all the way through 1968, when it was lowered to 10 inches.

While diamond dimensions have changed little in the last century and a half, the outfield distances at Wrigley Field fluctuated during the park's first decades. The deepest part of the

*Grounds crew preparing the field, with crew chief Bobby Dorr in suit*

field in center sat 440 feet from home plate when Weeghman Park opened in 1914, and the left- and right-field foul lines extended 345 feet and 356 feet, respectively. Following modifications to the outfield seating areas, the foul lines ran just 327 and 321 feet by the time the Cubs moved in, in 1916. Right field became as short as 298 feet in 1921 to accommodate more fans, but a major renovation to the ballpark's configuration in 1922 pushed the right-field distance back to 399 feet. More seating was installed later in the 1920s, and the fence returned to a more manageable 321 feet away. The renovation of 1938 gave Wrigley the dimensions it holds to this day: 355 feet to the left-field foul pole, 368 feet to the power alleys, 400 feet to center, and 353 down the right-field line.

*Grounds crew preparing the field, Opening Day, 2006*

# DUGOUTS AND CLUBHOUSES

In the young days of Chicago baseball, players on the sidelines usually sat or stood in a bench area near the grandstand, with little or no protection from the weather or unruly fans. By the 1880s, ballparks had more sheltered, if still a bit rickety, spaces for the players' bench. West Side Grounds, which opened in 1893, featured covered shelters in front of the grandstands—Fred Tenney of the Boston Beaneaters is shown ducking out from the visitors' dugout during a 1906 game against the Cubs—although the dugout was not, in fact, dug out of the ground. The configuration and size of the dugouts changed as adjustments were made to the grandstand seating areas along the foul lines, and by 1910, the dugout was a permanent fixture within West Side Grounds.

The early dugouts at Wrigley Field had canopies that could be unrolled to provide protective cover for the benches. Throughout the first few decades, however, the dugouts still offered little room for equipment, so bats and gloves and whatever else were laid in front of the dugout steps.

The first clubhouse facilities at Wrigley also lacked much in the way of luxuries, offering a locker and wooden chair for each player. Team trainer Andy Lotshaw had the job of packing up the equipment from the locker room before the team headed off for spring training.

Wrigley's modern dugouts retain the classic wooden benches (eschewing padded seats), but the additional storage space for equipment and a healthy stock of snacks and beverages offer modern comforts and conveniences. In 2006, Wrigley went high-tech with the installation of wireless communication systems between the dugouts and bullpens. Country music recording artist Trace Adkins got a chance to relax in the dugout with manager Lou Piniella and the players before Adkins sang the national anthem at a game in 2007.

*Fred Tenney and Boston Beaneaters in dugout, West Side Grounds, 1906*

*Cubs players in dugout, Wrigley Field, 1929*

*Andy Lotshaw in clubhouse, Wrigley Field, 1926*

*Singer Trace Adkins and Cubs in dugout, 2007*

# BULLPENS

The origin of the term "bullpen" has several possible explanations. One theory says the term arose in the early years of the National League when late-arriving fans, who were offered discount tickets if they showed up after the first inning, were penned in like bulls behind ropes in foul territory. This was also the area where pitchers warmed up before games. Another story has the term deriving from the Bull Durham tobacco billboards that were ubiquitous at ballparks a century ago. Whatever the origin, the term came into popular parlance by the 1910s.

Like the dugout, the pitchers' area has also improved in amenities through the ages. The first Cubs hurlers had little more than a designated patch of dirt on the sidelines between the dugout and home plate, where they could loosen up the old arm before the game.

While many ballparks have bullpens located behind the outfield wall, at Wrigley the relievers are in plain sight of the crowd along the first- and third-base foul ground. It may be humble surroundings, but other than a place to sit and some refreshments, what more could you really want on a summer day at the park?

**Right:** *Fergie Jenkins warming up in the bullpen, 1971*
**Below:** *Mark Prior warming up in the bullpen, 2004*

*Russ Meyer warming up in the bullpen, circa 1948*

# Programs and Scorecards

For the fan settling into a seat at the ballpark, nothing sets the stage better than the game program and scorecard, along with a hot dog and an icy cold beverage. The program has been a fan favorite since the very early days of the sport. Cap Anson struck a regal pose for the cover of Chicago's official 1892 scorecard. For the price of a nickel, fans could keep score from the stands, find out about upcoming games, and peruse a plethora of ads from local merchants. Eight decades later, the scorecard hadn't changed much. The two-page fold-out in 1971—still just 15 cents—included the team rosters, ticket info and schedules, and a menu of snack and souvenir items available at Wrigley.

Today's game program still offers complete rosters, stats, and plenty of advertisements. For the fan who wants (and is willing to pay) a little more, the "Official Yearbook-Style Program" is a hefty 160-page bonanza of all things Cubs, with spotlights on players, promotional events, and a team gallery. A fresh scorecard is included, of course, and the program would not be complete without plenty of baseball-oriented advertisements, like the team's official ketchup and a tantalizing bottle of Budweiser.

*Scorecard cover, 1892*

*Scorecard interior, 1971*

*Scorecard cover, 2007*

# TAKE ME OUT TO THE BALLGAME

Chicago fans have long had an insatiable craving for their home team, and not surprisingly, the fan base reaches a peak when the team is playing well. During the dynasty years a century ago, the Cubs were consistently a top attraction, finishing first or second in attendance among National League teams in every season from 1902 to 1912. In 1926, the franchise began a string of seven years at the top of the league attendance, and in 1927, it became the first NL team to bring in more than a million fans in a season.

Despite playing in one of the smaller ballparks in the majors (41,160 is the official capacity), the Cubs continue to be a top-drawing team. More than three million fans visited Wrigley in every season from 2004 through 2007, with a franchise-record 3,252,462 passing through the turnstiles in 2007.

Long lines at the ticket booths have been a regular sight at Wrigley Field and its predecessors for more than a century. In the days before internet sales, thousands of tickets were sold over the phone as well as at the park. Wrigley Field ticket manager George Doyle and his assistant worked feverishly to keep pace with incoming calls for tickets from excitable Cubs fans, a month before the start of the 1937 season.

In September of 1998, Cubs fans sprinted to Wrigley Field for a chance to buy a ticket to a one-game playoff against the San

*Ticket manager George Doyle and assistant, Wrigley Field ticket office, 1937*

Francisco Giants to determine the Wild Card team in the National League playoffs. Tickets were gone as quickly as they could be handed out, but huge numbers returned to the ticket booth on game day to stand in long lines in hopes of getting a standing-room ticket. To the delight of 39,556 fans at Wrigley Field (official capacity at the time was 38,902), the Cubs beat the Giants 5-3 and advanced to the playoffs for the first time in nearly a decade.

In the early days of Chicago baseball, a day at the ballpark was an intimate affair. Lakefront Park had seating for only about 3,000 people, and Wrigley Field (Weeghman Park) could accommodate only 14,000 spectators in its original 1914 incarnation—barely one-third of what it can hold today. Then again, back in the old days, teams were happy to pack hundreds more into every ballpark nook and cranny, particularly for big games. The club set up temporary seating areas in front of the grandstands and bleachers, and spectators could watch from roped-off areas on the edges of the playing field itself. For the 1912 City Series between the Cubs and White Sox, fans were crowded in close to the action alongside the dugouts and in front of the outfield wall at West Side Grounds. Even as late as the 1930s, overflow fans were permitted to sit or stand on the outskirts of the field for an up-close view of the action. Fans also had a chance to

*Line at ticket window, West Side Grounds, 1908*

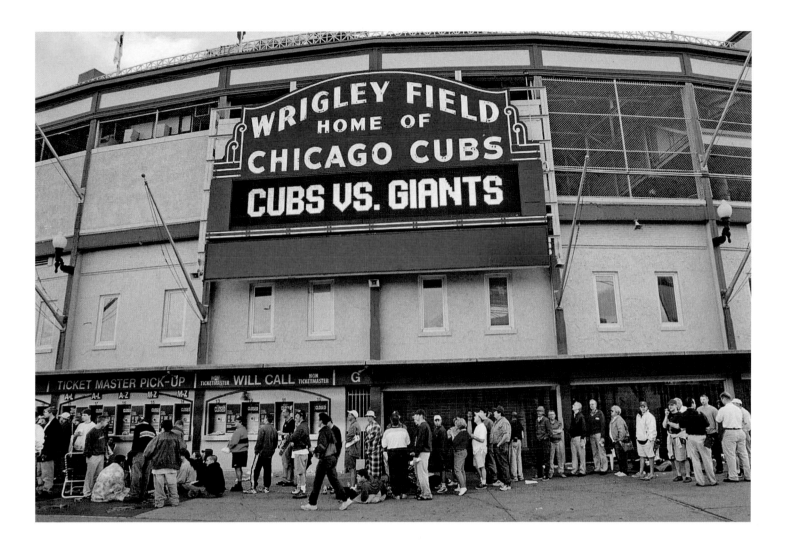

**Above:** *Ticket line for playoff game, Wrigley Field, 1998*

**Left:** *Fan entering Wrigley Field, Opening Day, 2004*

tread where their heroes tread on the field on their way out of the ballpark after the game.

Generations later—while any fan who comes onto the field is sure to get expelled from the game and hauled away by the cops—the ballpark still attracts enormous numbers of spectators. A crowd of 41,364 came out to the Friendly Confines to watch the Cubs take on the Pittsburgh Pirates in the final home game of the 2007 regular season. Best of all, those in attendance got to witness the Cubs blow away the opposition with an 8-0 victory and inch closer to clinching the division crown.

To attend that afternoon game in 2007, a family of four could easily shell out several hundred dollars for good seats, plus snacks and souvenirs. A hundred years earlier, a ticket for a box seat might set you back a little over a dollar; a bleacher seat could be had for just two bits. The cheapest seat at Wrigley today, in the corners of the upper deck, is $16 for most games or $8 for selected "value" games. Prices rise quickly from there. Standard box seats in the infield run you close to $60, and a first-class view from behind home plate or next to the dugout can cost as much as $250 for a "prime" game. To sit in the storied Wrigley Field outfield bleachers, it's $32 for a general admission ticket. The luxurious private suites bring in big revenue for the club, and 50 of your best friends can cheer on the Cubbies from the Grand Slam Suite for around $10,000.

*Crowd at City Series, West Side Grounds, 1912*

*Season finale, Wrigley Field, 2007*

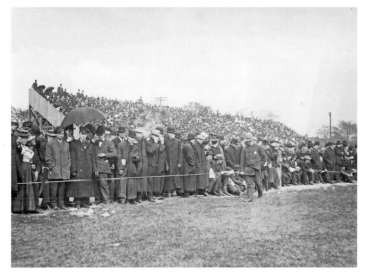

*Spectators on edge of field, West Side Grounds, 1907*

*Fans exiting Wrigley Field, 1930s*

# THE FANS

For many Cubs supporters, going out to the old ballgame is simply a pleasant way to spend a summer's afternoon or evening. For others, it's an all-day event involving painted faces, huge banners, and all-out support for the home team. Dating back to the old West Side Grounds, men and women of all ages would come out and cheer on the successes and bemoan the failures of their hometown boys. Even in the chilly weather of early April or (if all goes well) October, the faithful will show up for their Cubbies.

Even as the team was bringing in big crowds in the 1920s, owner William Wrigley and president Bill Veeck Sr. sought to attract more of the "fairer sex" to the ballpark (and boost attendance). So, they instituted Ladies' Day, offering free admittance to all women. On June 27, 1930, a record crowd of 51,556 showed up to see Chicago defeat the Brooklyn Dodgers—since it was Ladies' Day, only 19,748 of those fans paid for their tickets.

*Cubs Rooters Club, West Side Grounds, 1908*

*Ladies' Day, Wrigley Field, 1930s*

**CHICAGO CUBS**

**LADIES DAY TICKET**

We are happy to welcome you to Wrigley Field as our guest, subject to the conditions on the back of this ticket.

Just A Reminder—You can buy a comfortable, reserved box seat for only $1.25 at the exchange booth inside the park.

**CHICAGO NATIONAL LEAGUE BALL CLUB**

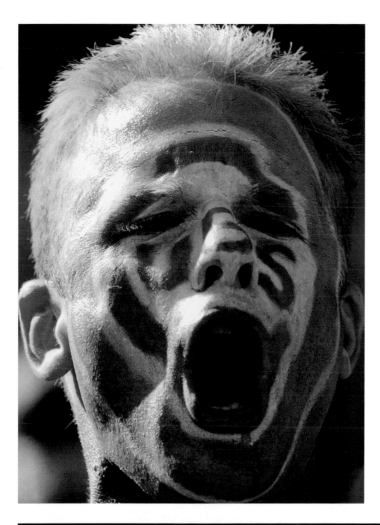

**Above:** *Fans keeping warm, April 2003*

**Left**: *Fan showing his true colors, 2003 National League Championship Series*

*Fans showing their support, September 2007*

Over the years, the men in white and blue have shown their appreciation by indulging loyal fans with an autograph or a simple shake of the hand. From legends like Phil Cavarretta to up-and-comers like pitcher Sean Marshall, an autograph from a favorite Cub is a priceless souvenir.

The storied Cubs franchise has long attracted well-known faces to its grandstand seats as well. President William H. Taft—a passionate baseball fan and initiator of the tradition of presidential first pitches on Opening Day—received lots of attention from the crowd when he attended a game at the West Side Grounds in 1909. In more recent times, guests of honor at Wrigley Field have included everyone from presidents Ronald Reagan and Bill Clinton to comedians Will Ferrell and Bill Murray, who tossed the ball over the backstop during his ceremonial first pitch at a game in April 2004. In his youth, Reagan had broadcast Cubs games in simulation on WHO radio in Des Moines, Iowa, beginning in 1933, until he decided to pursue a career in acting in 1937.

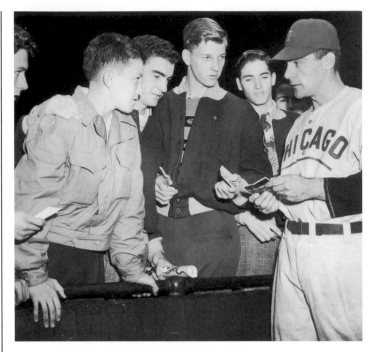

*Phil Cavarretta signing autographs, circa 1946*

*Sean Marshall signing autographs, 2007*

*President William H. Taft, West Side Grounds, 1909*

*President Ronald Reagan, Wrigley Field, 1988*

*Bill Murray, Wrigley Field, 2004*

# WILDCAT BLEACHERS

With the Cubs being such a hot attraction, fans have long sought ways to catch a free glimpse of the action. The buildings across the street from West Side Grounds were popular vantage points from which to sneak a peak at the field, and by 1907, many building owners had constructed full-fledged bleachers on the roof. During the 1907 World Series, fans latched on to any available space they could to watch the game, straddling the ballpark's back walls, climbing parapets and chimneys, and hanging from telephone poles. Owner Charles Murphy did what he could to put that to an end by increasing the heights of the outer walls surrounding the park.

This tradition of wildcat bleachers continued with equal fervor when the team moved eight miles north to the intersection of Addison and Clark. The buildings on Waveland and Sheffield Avenues beyond left and right field offered prime views inside Wrigley. Here, too, the owners of neighboring buildings saw this as an opportunity and provided regular seating on the rooftops. The Cubs front office tolerated the arrangement for many years, but when the bleachers became more permanent and the building owners began charging admission and selling refreshments, the team felt things had gone too far. Threatening legal action, the organization erected dark green screens above the outfield bleachers that obscured the views from across the

*Dark windscreens obscuring the view into Wrigley Field, 2002*

street. A truce was ultimately reached, and the building owners agreed to share a portion of their proceeds with the team. This standoff also led to the neighborhood's blessing for the Cubs to expand the bleacher sections of the ballpark, extending them over the sidewalks on Waveland and Sheffield.

*West Side Grounds, 1907 World Series*

*Fans watch from rooftop bleachers on Waveland Avenue, 2001*

# Game Day Snacks

The first permanent concession stand in baseball was installed at Wrigley Field in 1914. Today, it's almost impossible to imagine a day at the ballpark without hot dogs, peanuts, popcorn, and a cold refreshing beverage. In baseball's younger days, small armies of vendors strolled the aisles selling snacks and drinks; if you had a craving, cigarette girls would deliver a pack right to your seat. The introduction of a "smoky links" cart was big news at the stadium in the late 1930s—and what respectable wiener doesn't taste better with an ice-cold beer? Game programs would advertise the available brews and other enticing treats.

While the traditional favorites like popcorn and peanuts, hot dogs, and beer are still the big sellers, today's fans mob food stands all around the park, gobbling up full menus of delicacies from far and wide, including seafood, Asian cuisine, authentic Mexican food, and microbrews. A 40-cent beer might be a thing of the past, but game-day feasts, and fans' gusto for them, are as much a part of today's ballpark experience as ever before.

*Hot dog vendor, Wrigley Field*

*Concession stand, Wrigley Field*

*Popcorn vendors, Wrigley Field*

*Cigarette girl, Wrigley Field*

*Beer vendor, Wrigley Field, 2002*

# VOICES OF THE CUBS

As with many of the game's traditions, the Chicago Cubs were pioneers in taking baseball to the airwaves. In the mid-1920s, other owners scoffed when William Wrigley Jr. announced his plan to broadcast Cubs games over the radio. Skeptics warned that the ballpark would be empty if fans could follow the action at home for free. Wrigley and Bill Veeck Sr., however, believed that it would raise interest in the team and draw more people to the ballpark. They were right. Attendance at Wrigley Field soared. By 1935, every Cubs home game could be heard on as many as five different stations.

Since then, Chicago has had a rich legacy of iconic broadcasters, four of whom were honored by the Baseball Hall of Fame with the annual Ford C. Frick Award for excellence in broadcasting: Bob Elson, Jack Brickhouse, Milo Hamilton, and Harry Caray.

Hal Totten was the first behind the mic, covering Cubs games from 1924 to 1944 for several stations, including WMAQ, WLS, WCFL, and WGN. Totten is credited as the first broadcaster to conduct on-field interviews with managers and players.

Illinois native Jack Brickhouse began his broadcasting career in 1934 at WMBD radio in Peoria when he was only 18 years old. He was hired by WGN radio in 1940 and seven years later became

*Jack Brickhouse, Wrigley Field broadcast booth, 1979*

the face of the Cubs when games first hit television. (Three stations televised the Cubs during the first few seasons, until WGN secured exclusive rights in 1952.) Covering both the Cubs and White Sox until 1967, then exclusively the Cubs, "Brick" had an infectious enthusiasm for the game and his team. Reflecting on the Cubs' long dry spell in postseason play, Brickhouse once remarked, "Anyone can have a bad century." He broadcast his five thousandth game for WGN in August of 1979 and retired two years later. His trademark "Hey-hey" after a home-team homer still echoes in the memories of many Cubs fans.

Vince Lloyd was Brickhouse's partner on WGN-TV during the 1950s and early 1960s until Lloyd moved to the radio booth, where he stayed for 23 years. Lloyd's radio partner was former All-Star player Lou Boudreau. Boudreau first joined the WGN team in 1958, and other than a one-year shift as manager in 1960, he was the voice of the Cubs until 1987.

Longtime and much-beloved announcer Harry Caray took Brickhouse's spot on TV in 1982, after many years calling games for the St. Louis Cardinals and White Sox. Despite his previous history with the Cubs' two biggest rivals, Caray quickly became a fan favorite on Chicago's North Side. With WGN's expansion as a cable superstation, Caray's colorful and outspoken approach was telecast across the country. Great Cubs plays were celebrated with the classic Caray-ism, "Holy cow!" At the ballpark, his "Take Me Out to the Ball Game"

*Hal Totten, with Charlie Grimm, Woody English, and Lon Warneke, 1933*

sing-along during the seventh-inning stretch was an institution. When Caray passed away in 1998, his funeral was one of the most-attended in Chicago history. The Cubs continue to honor Caray's legacy by inviting guest performers, ranging from Hillary Clinton to Ozzy Osbourne, to lead the home crowd in the singing of "Take Me Out to the Ballgame." A caricature of Harry Caray hangs near the broadcast booth and a statue of him stands outside the ballpark.

Caray's grandson Chip worked with Harry in the elder's final year and stayed on as a Cubs broadcaster until 2004. (He left to work at the TBS superstation, where he teamed with his father, Harry's son Skip Caray.)

Steve Stone worked alongside both Carays during his 20-year tenure as color analyst for WGN-TV. Stone generated a lot of controversy by openly criticizing Cubs players and manager Dusty Baker during the 2004 season, and he retired that November. The Cubs hired Bob Brenly to replace Stone, and two weeks later Len Kasper was hired to replace Chip Caray as the play-by-play man.

A fan favorite when he manned third base, Ron Santo has been a favorite in the radio booth since 1990. He has suffered from diabetes, heart disease, and cancer, but he continues to bring his enthusiasm to every Cubs game. Pat Hughes has been Santo's on-air partner since 1996, and "Pat and Ron" are a highlight for listeners throughout Cubs country.

*Lou Boudreau, with Burt Hooten, 1974*

*Harry Caray, Wrigley Field broadcast booth*

*Ron Santo (left) with Pat Hughes, 1999*

# SPRING TRAINING

If it's spring, we're talkin' baseball. After a long winter of hibernation, spring training is the annual rite of passage to the season for players and fans alike. It's a chance for the team to work on the fundamentals and for fans to kick back in the sunshine and catch a sneak peak at their heroes.

During the first few decades of the twentieth century, the Cubs ventured to an assortment of sunny locales for early-season practice, including Los Angeles, Pasadena, Santa Monica, New Orleans, Tampa, and Hot Springs, Arkansas. Beginning in 1921, Catalina Island was the team's annual warm-weather escape from Chicago's frigid winters. William Wrigley Jr. owned the island, located 20 miles southwest of Los Angeles, and he had a ballpark built with the same dimensions as the field back home.

*Spring training at Catalina Island, 1920s*

*Cubs rookies at Catalina Island, circa 1935*

*Cubs at Catalina Island, 1920s*

He also built a clubhouse for his team; the clubhouse stands today as part of the Catalina Country Club. Between drills and scrimmages, the players could enjoy a swim in the ocean or even a horseback ride.

In 1952, the team moved its spring training to Mesa, Arizona. With the exception of a one-year hiatus to Long Beach in 1966 and an 11-year stand in Scottsdale (1967–1978), the Cubs have made Mesa their preseason destination for most of the last half century. During the first stint in Mesa, the team played at Rendezvous Park. Since 1979, they have made their springtime home at two different ballparks at HoHoKam Park. HoHoKam is a Native American term loosely translated as "those who vanished"—not an allusion to the team's performance in October but rather the name of the organization that enticed the Cubs to Arizona and that continues to maintain the park. The first HoHoKam was razed in 1996 and replaced with a new, 12,500-seat facility. The Cubs regularly set spring-training attendance records at the spacious park. HoHoKam has the same outfield dimensions as Wrigley Field, and it serves duty as a minor league park when the Cubs aren't using it. The field offers perks such as well-furnished clubhouses, multiple practice fields, batting tunnels and cages, and extensive exercise and training equipment, all below the bright Arizona sun.

*HoHoKam Park, March 2006*

*Spring training, February 2007*

*Pitchers (left to right) Carlos Zambrano, Will Ohman, Scott Eyre, and Mark Prior loosening up at spring training, February 2007*

# At the Farm

In the early days of organized baseball, major league teams lacked any formal minor league affiliations. Minor league players would simply be sold to the highest bidder. The advent of affiliates created a system in which organizations could develop talent for the big league club. One of the earliest and longest-lasting associations for the Chicago Cubs was the Los Angeles Angels of the Pacific Coast League. William Wrigley purchased the Angels in 1921, and in 1932, they became formally affiliated, a relationship that lasted until 1957. The Angels' home field, also known as Wrigley Field, was a gem of the minor leagues. (Indeed, it carried the name Wrigley Field a year before the parent's ballpark, which was still known as Cubs Park when the minor league field opened in 1925.)

In the 1940s, Cubs general manger Jim Gallagher encouraged P. K. Wrigley to expand the team's farm system, and by 1947, the club had as many as 20 minor league affiliates. There was a lot of turnover in the ranks, and some teams served as affiliates for just a season or two, while others remained in the Cubs family for as long as a decade. The teams were based in all corners of the country—from Tacoma, Washington, to St. Augustine, Florida, and from Springfield, Massachusetts, to Visalia, California—as well as throughout the Midwest in Illinois, Iowa, and Wisconsin.

*Kerry Wood, Iowa Cubs, 2006*

Since the late 1950s, the number of affiliates has ranged from three to seven. The Iowa Cubs have been a part of the system since 1981. The Triple-A team plays in Des Moines and is a popular attraction for the surrounding community. It is also a common stopover for big league stars working their way back from injury, such as Kerry Wood, who went to Des Moines in May 2006 to help rehab his shoulder following arthroscopic surgery.

At the lower levels, the Peoria Chiefs, of the Single-A Midwest League, were a Chicago affiliate from 1985 to 1995 before taking a nine-year hiatus with the Cardinals system. They rejoined the Cubs ranks in 2005. Among the names that have appeared on Chiefs jerseys over the years are Greg Maddux, Rafael Palmeiro, and Mark Grace. In 2007, Peoria hired Ryne Sandberg as its manager, bringing a franchise legend back into the fold. The Daytona Cubs of the Single-A Florida State League play at scenic Jackie Robinson Ballpark. Daytona has won two league titles since the team was established in 1993 as a Cubs affiliate.

*Wrigley Field, Los Angeles, 1930s*

*Ryne Sandberg, Peoria Chiefs manager, 2007*

*Daytona Cubs game, Jackie Robinson Ballpark, 2006*

# BIBLIOGRAPHY AND RESOURCES

Ahrens, Art, and Edward Gold. *Day by Day in Chicago Cubs History*. New York: Leisure Press, 1982.

Dewey, Donald, and Nicholas Acocella. *Ball Clubs: Every Franchise, Past and Present, Officially Recognized by Major League Baseball*. Toronto: SportClassic Books, 2005.

Gentile, Derek. *The Complete Chicago Cubs*. New York: Black Dog & Leventhal, 2002.

Gillette, Gary, and Pete Palmer. *The ESPN Baseball Encyclopedia*. 4th ed. New York: Sterling, 2007.

Leventhal, Josh. *Baseball Yesterday & Today*. St. Paul, Voyageur Press, 2006.

Snyder, John. *Cubs Journal*. Cincinnati: Emmis Books, 2005.

**Websites**

www.cubs.mlb.com

www.chicagocubsonline.com

www.baseballreference.com

www.baseballlibrary.com

www.thebaseballpage.com

# INDEX